Second CHANCES

Second
CHANCES

The ULTIMATE GUIDE to THRIFTING, SUSTAINABLE STYLE, and EXPRESSING Your Most AUTHENTIC SELF

MACY ELENI

SIMON ELEMENT

New York London Toronto
Sydney New Delhi

SIMON
ELEMENT

An Imprint of Simon & Schuster, LLC
1230 Avenue of the Americas
New York, NY 10020

First Simon Element trade paperback edition
September 2024

SIMON ELEMENT is a trademark of
Simon & Schuster, LLC

Simon & Schuster:
Celebrating 100 Years of Publishing in 2024

For information about special discounts for bulk
purchases, please contact Simon & Schuster
Special Sales at 1-866-506-1949 or business@
simonandschuster.com.

The Simon & Schuster Speakers Bureau can bring
authors to your live event. For more information
or to book an event, contact the Simon & Schuster
Speakers Bureau at 1-866-248-3049 or visit our
website at www.simonspeakers.com.

Cover and Book Design by
Shubhani Sarkar, sarkardesignstudio.com

Manufactured in China

10 9 8 7 6 5 4 3 2 1

Library of Congress Cataloging-in-Publication Data
has been applied for.

ISBN 978-1-6680-3136-0

ISBN 978-1-6680-3137-7 (ebook)

I dedicate this book to

The entire thrift community and all lovers of used things. YOU are my heart and soul, and the first people to accept me exactly as I am.

My thrift queens and beans that have been on this journey with me since the very beginning and always supported my dream to tell stories through old clothes. Our bond is so special to me, and I feel beyond blessed to have all of your fabulous faces a part of my world.

My younger self. I'm so grateful you held on for the good stuff, I told you it'd be worth it!

And in beyond loving memory of my grandpa William Evans, who introduced me to storytelling, physically cut out and sent me the style section of the *New York Times* every single Sunday, and believed in me for being me. You were the best grandpa a little girl could have ever asked for and made space for me to always keep dreaming. I felt you with me as I wrote every word of this book, and I will carry the kindness and empathy you always exuded to others with me for the rest of my life.

CONTENTS

INTRODUCTION

SECONDHAND SHOPPING HAS NEVER BEEN MORE POPULAR. FOR ME, THAT SPARK WAS IGNITED WELL over a decade ago.

In my world, fashion has always involved thrifting. I was raised by the truest of superheroes—a single mom in Dayton, Ohio—and spent every Wednesday and countless weekends at my local Salvation Army. I'd roll through the aisles, comb through each rack, and go home to throw my finds in the wash, followed by endless hours of playing dress-up. I was captivated by the idea that one store could make all my fashion dreams come to life. And the best part? I could afford it! I'd found my home away from home, a place that transported me from a a far-less-than-sparkly reality to another world. A world where, for a few minutes or, most of the time, hours, it was just me, my imagination, and the clothes. There was no judgment, there were no rules. Experimentation and exploration were more than encouraged—they were necessary! For a really long time, the clothes were what kept me going. Never did I think that, more than ten years later, my love for digging out true fashion diamonds among the rough would lead me to my dream career with an audience of millions cheering me on virtually, as opposed to my mom and sister applauding my finds in the basement of our suburban home.

Over the past few years, interest in the secondhand shopping world has grown an insane amount. Thrifting, or the purchasing of used goods, is making its way to the forefront of daily dressing for many. As costs rise on literally everything and the concept of sustainability becomes a much larger part of the global conversation, giving new life to pieces tossed away by others is becoming much more the norm. And I am so excited for the secondhand fashion movement to finally have its shining moment.

Growing up in Ohio, I felt incredibly removed from the world of fashion. It was this shimmery universe in a faraway land that I only saw depicted in the glossy pages of my cherished childhood magazines. This lack of access prompted me to dive headfirst into research in the nascent days of Google. On a typically gray Ohio day, there on my computer screen, I found Tavi Gevinson on BlogSpot .com. Tavi, who was just a few years younger than I, was uploading her daily outfits (groundbreaking, I know, but, TBH, in 2010 it was!) to her blog, *Style Rookie*. She donned "granny" floral prints, layered upon crazy vintage knits, topped with a massive bow adding feet to her tiny preteen stature. She was one of the OG fashion maximalists before there was a hashtag for it. Even though our personal styles were vastly different, her use of clothing as a vessel for storytelling and self-expression was mesmerizing. I had been looking for something, anything, that allowed me to dream outside the constraints of my hometown, and Tavi felt like my own little secret. Actually, at the time, the whole internet felt like my little secret as no one at my high school ever knew what I was going on about. As I stumbled upon the first wave of YouTube fashion vloggers, I realized that there were others out there who, themselves, were craving that same connection and space to share their love for style just as much as I was. If I knew anything, it was that I loved the camera, I loved storytelling, and I *loved* clothes. At that very moment, I decided to create my first-ever YouTube channel under the name "fashionoutsider09"—remember, this was a time when we didn't yet know if it was safe to put our real names on the internet. This is when I realized that, with the click of a button, I could be transported from my bedroom in Ohio to a place that felt so much more like home.

———

I was diagnosed with depression and anxiety at a pretty young age, and therefore spent a lot of my adolescent days down in le dumps. I was battling demons that presented themselves as an ongoing internal dialogue, convincing me I was never good enough. When I think back to my teen years in the mid-2000s, I see a little lost me, with far too much hair spray and a shit ton of eyeliner, sitting on

my bed in the basement of my mother's house, walls covered from floor to ceiling with spreads ripped from the pages of countless issues of *Teen Vogue*, *Seventeen*, and *Nylon*. At that time, so many aspects of my life stripped me of joy, but the few hours a week I could spend at my local thrift store, re-creating the looks from the pages covering my walls, gave me an escape. When I walked through those squeaky red Salvation Army doors, it was like everything else went quiet and I was able to just be me.

Free of judgment from the not-so-kind girls at school who thought used clothing was gross and made sure I knew it, or my extremely narcissistic father, who had me questioning my worth daily. The thrift store gave me the power to make my own magic and I wanted to harness it forever.

I remember the first time I ever realized that thrifting was my superpower. I had applied for *Teen Vogue*'s Fashion University, a summit of sorts being held over a long weekend in New York City. There, teens from across the country would gather in person to hear from industry leaders and insiders, such as Zac Posen, Vera Wang, and even Anna Wintour, the editor in chief of *Vogue*. The application was simple, just an essay on why they should choose YOU

to attend this iconic event and a series of photos that showed off your personal style. I whipped that essay up no problem but was overwhelmed thinking about how exactly I would throw together just the right fits to convince whoever those "fashion judges" were that I, Macy Eleni from Dayton, Ohio, was worthy of this experience. Nothing had ever been more exciting to me than the idea of getting out of Ohio, even for just a few days, and being allowed access to the glamorous world of fashion. I wanted to learn, I wanted to grow, I wanted to be surrounded by people who also felt so completely moved, transported, and captivated by clothing. So,

SECOND CHANCES

in true Macy fashion, I went right to the thrift store and dug out some pieces dripping in 2010 Ke$ha meets Forever 21 energy, then had my little sister (and forever partner in crime) Lexy hang up a white sheet in our basement, where we snapped photos all night long.

I turned in my application and was accepted into the program a few weeks later. At that moment, I felt really, really cool about my secondhand clothes. They, along with my witty words, had gotten me there and I knew they'd continue to carry me throughout the rest of my life.

And they have done just that. Over the years that followed, I went through my fair share of ups and downs. I graduated from high school, had an abortion, went to college, met the love of my life, struggled through an eating disorder, gained friends, and lost loved ones so near and dear to my heart. I dreamed every single day of a life outside of Ohio and I did it all in thrifted clothing. I knew from such a young age that storytelling and connecting with others was what I was here on this silly little planet to do. I didn't know how I was going to do it, but I had such a strong feeling, deep in my gut, that I could make all my dreams come true and do it by being myself.

I moved out to Los Angeles in the winter of 2017 with no job, no connections, no friends, no family . . . just my partner of the past decade, Tyler, and a car we drove across the country packed to the gills with all our belongings. I spent those first few years in LA as an absolute mess. But, as I would come to learn, sometimes the mess is exactly what makes room for true magic, kind of like the Goodwill bins but we'll get into that later! I was working the reception desk at a tanning salon in Beverly Hills, where my boss was a nasty misogynist, who also paid us below minimum wage. I literally dreaded going into work every day. During that time, I had also made the decision to enter recovery for an eating disorder I had been suffering from since I was around six years old. I was desperately sick of caring so much about how small I could make myself. Nope, not anymore! I wanted to treat myself right, be my own biggest cheerleader, and go after the life I knew I deserved.

Fast-forward to July 2020. At this point, we had all been trapped inside for months because of the coronavirus and I was in such a deep creative slump. I viciously wrote in my *gratitudy booty journal* every day, mapping out the life I knew could and would be mine, but I still had no clue how I was going to set it in motion, especially when we could barely even leave the house, but I wrote it out anyway . . . every single dream I had for myself.

I had been sharing my thrift trips and tips on YouTube under the name Blazed and Glazed for a few months before the pandemic hit but didn't feel like I was fully tapping into my potential or finding my people. I had so much to say, so much to share, and I wanted to create a space in the virtual world of fashion where it felt like everyone belonged. A place where you don't need a lot of money, or to be close to a big city, or dripping in designer duds. I wanted to take my experience of feeling like a fashion "outsider" and use it to create space for others just like me. But first, I had to make my way to the elusive table.

That July, Tyler suggested I try out TikTok, and since I truly had nothing to lose, I hit upload and my life was changed forever. My first video to go viral was a simple forty-eight-second *thrift haul*. I stood in my living room and showed just six items I had picked up that afternoon from the Out of the Closet thrift store, an incredible spot in West Hollywood where the majority of profits are used to raise funds for the AIDS Healthcare Foundation. That one little post revealed to me just how many people were either 1) as obsessed with used clothing as I was, or 2) had never even thought to set foot in a thrift store and were flabbergasted by the fact that I had just whipped out not one but *two* Helmut Lang dresses for only five dollars a pop. From that day on I've uploaded countless videos a week on thrifting, estate sales, self-expression, and my continuous battles with endometriosis, depression, and anxiety. I began highlighting my most iconic thrift scores and sharing how I personally practice positive thinking, which definitely doesn't come naturally to me. What followed has truly been the greatest blessing of my life thus far, finding you guys, finding myself, sharing my story and, of course, all my fabulous finds! I was profiled in *Nylon* later that year, one of the very magazines that covered my walls as a teen, to discuss my journey and love of all things used. That full-circle moment proved to me that I could do anything in my thrifted clothes, and I know you can too.

I've refered to my followers as "queens," but I don't think anyone really knows why . . . The truth is that Freddie Mercury, the late and beyond great lead singer of Queen, is one of my ultimate inspirations in life. Freddie was singing to the "misfits," the people standing in the back of the room who felt they didn't belong, but knew that they were exactly where they were meant to be. This perfectly describes the way I felt as I stumbled into fashion searching for that perfect fit—both literally and figuratively.

When I get your comments asking how I do it or, more importantly, how *you* can do it too, it lights my soul on fire. My high school self, who spent so much time thrifting alone, would be blown away by the sheer number of you who understand this passion I've been nurturing most of my life. To find other like-minded people who care about our world, the stories behind the garments we live our lives in, and who see secondhand clothing as a true vessel for stroytelling—that has meant everything to me. As I scroll through my DMs I find myself wishing I could jump in the car and take off on a magical secondhand journey, a trip to the thrift with each and every one of you! I want to run around the store, the flea, the estate sale, or be by your side as you scroll through never-ending listings on Poshmark looking for the cheapest Gucci kitten heels or the perfect pair of jeans. Since, sadly, that is impossible, I wanted to create something beyond my online presence, something tangible, inspiring . . . a tool to carry with you in your thrift bag as you navigate this trip into the universe of secondhand shopping. This book is for YOU! I'm spilling all my secrets on when, where, and *how* to transform into the ultimate *thrift queen*. This book is my love letter to thrifting and my way to give back to the community that has given me everything . . .

Okay, now let's shop!

Where TF DO I BEGIN?

SELECTING WHERE YOUR THRIFT MOMENT WILL TAKE PLACE IS CRUCIAL! THERE ARE A PLETHORA OF options to choose from and before we can go any further, we must break down the different types, vibes, and styles of secondhand shopping. These are the very spots, the treasure troves if you will, that will transform the way you think about clothing and introduce you to the magical experience of getting dressed in pieces that truly tell a story.

The CLASSIC Thrift Store

Let's kick this off with our classic, a tried-and-true *real-ass thrift store*! I'm talking endless racks, squeaky hangers, fluorescent lighting, and, possibly, staples used to attach the price tags to the clothes (btw, staples are very important . . . more on that later!). These are your Goodwills, Savers, Salvation Armys, but also and, TBH, more importantly, your local-run thrift stores. Those that give back to and aid the community through their profits. These are the spots that are going to give you options, baby, options! You'll have to spend some serious time there. But the feeling of finding the most unique pieces, unscorable elsewhere, makes all the time spent well worth it.

VINTAGE and Consignment Shops

Now, this is for my curated queens, those who simply don't have the time or maybe even the patience needed to successfully sift through the racks at that classic thrift. Maybe you're just looking to be more sustainable when it comes to your prom dress or next designer "treat yourself" moment. *Vintage shops*, like most everything in the secondhand shopping universe, are all vastly different and unique. Some spots will have a massive inventory with pieces from every decade, others will offer you an unimaginable selection of designer pieces from collections you didn't even know existed, while some will have a little bit of everything offering more accessible everyday price points. *Consignment shops* will even take your gently worn items in exchange for cash or store credit, which is a great way to keep that closet more *circular*. I have the most vivid memories

of pulling into the parking lot of the Miamisburg, Ohio, Plato's Closet. It was located in the dreariest strip mall and I rolled in once every two weeks to sell whatever I could scrounge up from my closet or sometimes my mom's or sister's (shhh, don't tell them!). I'd make just enough cash to run to the Dayton Mall, gather inspo, and drive straight to the thrift store. I loved being able to turn my clothes into . . . even more clothes.

1. Treasures of NYC   2. Wasteland Vintage   3. Voulez Vous Vintage   4. Wasteland Vintage

SECOND CHANCES

ESTATE Sales

Okay, *this* is where things get really crazy in the best way possible. For my newbies, an *estate sale* is a sale or auction to dispose of a substantial portion of the materials owned by a person who is recently deceased or who must dispose of their personal property to facilitate a move. In other words, it's a yard sale on speed, and for my queens ready to take their secondhand finds to the next level, yeah, estate sales are going to be your new obsession . . . and we'll chat all the tips you'll need to get started in chapter 8!

YARD Sales

While estate sales are fab and do take place all over the globe, I will admit that I am spoiled here in Los Angeles. Every weekend is a chance to explore the homes of Hollywood royalty or dig through the drawers of a seventies disco queen. I get it: the estates of Dayton, Ohio, or (insert your local small town here) may not offer that same level of glamour, but do not discount their magic! Much like our new bestie, the estate sale, they are filled with a specific person's or family's belongings, begging for a new home in which to live out their second or maybe even third life. Grab some cash, drive around your city, and search for signs (usually of the fluorescent nature) that will guide you in the right direction.

Tucked away in your neighbor's garage!

FLEA Markets

Much like yard sales, these babies take place all over, usually a street market with an assortment of different vendors. Here you'll find decades' worth of vintage clothing, usually a good amount of antique home décor, furniture, and quirky, fun knickknacks. Flea markets are also a great place to shop locally and support not only vintage sellers in your area but new emerging designers as well.

ANTIQUE Stores and Malls

Think of this as a flea market but indoors and usually dripping with knowledge and history. Some *antique* stores are on the smaller side, offering a more curated selection of true antique pieces and collectibles. Others are home to hundreds of vendors dealing vintage furniture, glassware, paintings, posters, magazines, mugs, jewelry, and yes, even fabulous clothes.

VIRTUAL RESALE Platforms

Resale platforms are nothing new and sites like eBay have been around carrying sexy secondhand style since the mid-1990s. However, with the rise of interest in thrifting, there have come to be endless ways to score from the comfort of your own home. I find some of my best vintage designer pieces (shoes, sunnies, bags, etc.) in the online thrifting world. Places like eBay, Poshmark, Whatnot, Depop, and ThredUp offer you the chance to shop closets from all over the globe.

The BINS

This is for my more experienced thrifters, who want to take it to the next level and really get down and dig. Goodwill outlet stores, or "*the bins*" as they are most frequently referred to, are a culmination of overflow donations, damaged items, and pieces that were on the floor for an extended period of time at a Goodwill store and did not sell. Think of this as the last stop before those items hit the landfill. The bins are cheaper than your average thrift store and usually operate off a pay-by-the-pound pay structure. Now, the bins can get wild and pretty competitive but they also hold space for major—and I mean *major*—scores to be had. Here are a few tips for this less conventional way of getting your hands on the goods.

- **EFFICIENCY IS KEY.** You're going to want to be hands-free at the bins, so empty your thrift bag into a fanny pack, and if you can only fit the bare minimum, take gloves, water, and a good-ass attitude. People are going to be moving around quickly and items will fall to the floor, so do yourself a solid and wear closed-toe shoes.

- **STAY CALM.** In the face of a large crowd or people getting a bit rowdy, remember that not everyone is after the same items as you and there is plenty to go around. As for the rowdiness, just keep in mind this is some people's full-time gig. A lot of resellers (which we'll chat more on in chapter 7) rely on the bins for their inventory, which can lead to a competitive vibe. Let them do their thing, stay kind, and get your search on!

- **GO HUNTING FOR MISSING PIECES!** Say you come across the top to a really fab vintage bikini or shoe you are totally gagged over and you let out a "Shit, where is its match?" Take a deep breath and don't give up hope. Chances are, the bottoms to the suit or the other shoe are buried in another bin, so take a lap around and look!

- **THROW IT ALL IN.** Fill your cart or bag with anything you think is up your alley and go through it all at the midpoint or the end of your bins excursion. Be really honest with yourself as to whether you truly like the item and have use for it or if you just want to snag it because of the low price point. Also, before purchasing the item, take time to check for damage, stains, etc., and have a plan in mind for how you would clean or repair it.

- **HAVE FUN!** Leave it up to the *thrift gods*. What is meant to find you will find you.

I challenge you to google "thrift stores near me," grab a reusable bag, put some gas in your car, and just hit every stop—but wait, first you're going to need tips!

ｃｔＥＲ

Tips to THRIFT BY

BELOW YOU WILL FIND MY PERSONAL MANIFESTO FOR HITTING THE RACKS AND PULLING OUT GOLD.

1. **Do your research!** As mentioned in the last chapter, it's crucial to do a bit of digging into what type of secondhand shop will meet your particular thrift needs. Refer back to the options listed in chapter 1 as a guide for where to go.

2. **Be in the mood,** especially if you are a beginner-level thrifter. Oftentimes, a good thrift adventure, be it ten minutes in a vintage spot or five hours at the Goodwill bins, can really aid in pulling me out of a funk. But if you're just simply not in the mood to sift, dig, and hunt, hold out for a day when you're feeling the vibes a bit more.

3. **Gather your inspiration** but don't let it cloud the search too much. It's good to have an ongoing list on hand of all your *thrift manifestations* and needs. This list will keep you focused and can act as a guide through the sections of the store. However, we have to remember that the thrift is always going to surprise us and will often deliver our desires in unconventional packages. Ones you may miss or pass up on because it doesn't directly match your inspo.

4. **Keep your mind open** and see an item for what it can be versus how it appears hanging on the rack (more on this in chapter 7).

5. **Check the days the store is open.** I know this probably sounds like common sense but in the world of secondhand shops (especially with a good chunk being small businesses or thrift spots run by religious organizations), some will be closed on Sundays and/or Mondays. Do yourself a favor and do a quick Google search before planning your excursion.

6. **Dress the part.** I do not mean plucking out the most stylish look from your wardrobe, but rather quite the opposite. Fitting rooms can be sparse

these days, so be sure to throw on an outfit made up of fewer layers, allowing you to slip things on and off with ease. To keep it comfortable, I usually opt for some flare leggings or biker shorts, a tank top, and a lightweight zip-up that can be tied around my waist if need be. Figure out whatever thrift uniform works best for you! And if you are on a specific thrift mission, bring along the pieces you may need to pair with the item you're searching for. (For example, are you thrifting a dress for a special occasion? Throw a pair of heels in your thrift bag! Either the ones you'll be specifically sporting the day of the occasion or a pair of a similar height. Have some specific pants that fit you like a damn glove but need a few more "new" pairs to sport? Bring them along for the hunt, so you can compare the fit/style to those on the racks at the thrift.)

7. **Curate the perfect playlist.** Now, this is a less tangible tip but it's important; trust me. I have been bopping out at the thrift store to the same "Morning Dance Party: Shimmy Shimmy, Let's Get It, Queens" playlist for years and I'm fully convinced it helps to bring me the goods. The tracks are strictly eighties pop and disco with a few Y2K bangers sprinkled in (Britney Spears, of course). I'm telling you, there is just something about throwback music that tells the thrift gods what you're looking for!

8. **Go early and often.** The *early bird* absolutely gets that hot designer find of a worm and I personally love a top-of-the-morning thrift trip. My preference is always me, the employees, the racks, and just a few other patrons. It's quiet, unpicked, and allows me to roll down aisle by aisle, flipping through every single item, in an efficient fashion. Get familiar with when the spots around you open and once you inevitably narrow in on your go-tos, I implore you to go as frequently as possible. I'm not saying you have to go every day but I do believe one of the biggest keys to an iconic thrift haul is spending as much time as you can familiarizing yourself with the thrift store. New merchandise is being put out on the floor (most places) minute by minute, so chances are what you see on the racks Monday will not be identical to what you find Wednesday or Saturday. Let this serve as your thrift queen reminder that to score the good-ass goodies you need to be in the thrift as much as possible. Don't let one *dry thrift* day deter you because the next could be the best thrift trip of your life.

9. **Location, location, location!** Where you're shopping can play a role in the aesthetic or decades you dig out. Palm Springs, California, a more retirement-based community than most, really delivers that eighties vacay feel. Tons of vintage swimwear, Tommy Bahama button-downs, jewel-tone tops: you get the vibe. A spot somewhere deep in, say, Montana is going to deliver more RealTree camo, cowgirl boots, and good-quality vintage denim. I cannot tell you how many times a day I hear "Of course your thrift finds are fabulous, you live in Los Angeles!" And while yes, Southern California does have some pretty phenomenal thrifting, I'd pick a small-town spot like the one nestled by my mom's house in Dayton, Ohio, over a big-city shop any day.

10. **Know your days!** There are three very important pieces to this specific thrift tip.

- Ask the employees at your local spots what day they do their big store restock on. This will mean a ton of new inventory on the floor that has yet to be searched through by others.

- Be aware of the color tags of the day. It's extremely common for thrift stores to use certain colors to price their merchandise and to have designated days that certain colors are an additional percent off. These days can be the difference between the same exact thrift haul being $15 as opposed to $50.

- Additionally, and this is different at every thrift store or chain, most spots are going to have designated days where a pretty thick discount is given to specific demographics. My mom's favorite thrift store does 50 percent for seniors every Monday, Savers does their own senior day with 30 percent off for those applicable on Tuesdays, and the Goodwills in Southern California have $1.99 Thursdays. Ask an employee or check the store's website and socials for what's good where you shop.

Which leads me to my next tip . . .

11. **Be kind to the employees!** You would think this goes without saying, but alas, we all know there are some who choose to be quite nasty or indifferent to those working in retail. But think of it like this: Those employed in the secondhand world are the keepers of the finds. They sort through the inventory, stock the racks, and can be the deciding factor in whether or not you get a personal price slash on a bruised item or a heads-up if they just got in some stellar brands. Also, they're just people doing their jobs, and I've seen far too many shoppers be unkind to thrift store employees. It's extremely uncool behavior, not thrift queen approved. (Flip to chapter 10 for more on creating a good relationship with your local thrift.)

12. **Don't be a vibe killer.** This is one of my biggest pet peeves when it comes to secondhand shopping as a whole. Everyone at the thrift store, vintage shop, estate sale, etc., is there for a different reason but we're all sharing the space and sifting through finds together. It aids absolutely no one (including yourself) to treat others poorly. So, much like we discussed above, be courteous of others shopping, especially those a bit on the older side or families with kids.

13. **Give the good to get the good!** In other words, donate! Thrift karma is extremely real and I am a firm believer that you must give the good shit to get the good shit. I like to give my current closet a little peep before hitting the thrift to see what is no longer being put to good use. If you aren't gravitating toward a certain wardrobe piece and it's still in pretty nice condition, consider how happy it could make someone else out on their own thrift mission. (We'll discuss the art of the thrifter's closet cleanout in chapter 6.)

14. **Shop "out of season."** Be on the lookout for items like coats and boots in the summer months. On the flip side, keep your eyes peeled for warm-weather staples like miniskirts, shorts, and sandals in the winter. Fewer people are shopping for those pieces when they're out of season, meaning you'll be able to score some really great items that would have otherwise been swooped up much faster.

15. **Thrifting is genderless.** I challenge you, no matter who you are or how you identify, to look in Every. Single. Section.

16. **Look through *all* sizes** because in the thrift store, as noted in the tip above, you never know what you will find or where you will find it. Most shoppers tend to put things back wherever they please, so there is a constant slew of items tagged as size small ending up in the large section and vice versa. I have also come to notice how inconsistent the size tags certain thrift spots attach to their garments can be. For example, the top could read clear as day a size large on its original brand tag but has been tagged a size small by the thrift store, and then stocked in the size small section on the rack.

17. **Never skip a "no pile."** All experienced thrifters know the pure magic that comes from another shopper's *"no pile"* and/or the *go-back rack* at the thrift store. There's a sheer rush of excitement that shimmies down your spine when you're having a dry thrift day and then stumble upon it, turning a trip from bland to grand in the blink of an eye. Made up of treasures a fellow thrift queen passed up and graciously left behind for you to score, these babies are most frequently found by the fitting rooms, mirrors, or near the ends of each rack.

18. **Touch everything.** I mean the fabrics, not the semi-questionable stains you're bound to come across when digging. Just by grabbing that little bit of the fabric, you'll often be able to tell if an item is itchy, falling apart, or *pilling*. On the flip side, you'll start to gain more knowledge on how to spot something more expensive and long-lasting like cashmere, leather, or silk.

19. **Don't be scared off by some damage.** Of course if an item is truly falling apart or stained beyond your level of repair, leave it behind. But if it is a garment you've long had on your thrift list or is just simply *so* you but has a small imperfection, snag it and flip to chapter 6.

20. **Check the insides of bags and shoes.** Much like inspecting the clothing pieces on the racks, I recommend always doing a more in-depth look through any purses or footwear you may have put in your cart. With bags, check for broken zippers, stuck snaps, rips to the interior, or even melted gum (less likely but I've seen it all). And when it comes to shoes of any type, *please* inspect the heels, outsoles, and insoles. Secondhand shoes can be tricky and I've experienced my fair share of iconic used shoes losing a heel in the most inconvenient of places. So do your thrift diligence and give that hot little score a serious once-over before heading to the register.

21. **Put everything you're feeling pulled to in your cart** and when you've reached the end of your search around the store, go through your loot item by item. First off, if you don't throw it in your cart, chances are someone else will. Second, it's easy to get super stoked on a find when you initially see it. You might love the brand but do you really love the top itself? It could be the shoe of your dreams but is it really your size? Do you want the hot party pants just because of the price point? Whatever that item is, pop it in your cart, continue to sift around the store, and wait till you've reached the end of your search to go through everything you've selected.

22. **Be picky!** For my thrift store newbies this one might be tough and you definitely shouldn't be hard on yourself for picking up a few flops in the beginning. But being picky about what gets to enter your personal wardrobe will help ease the work of getting dressed daily. As you're going through your cart of finds, pick up each piece, try it on if you can, look in the mirror, and attempt to picture how said item will work in your closet. This is where you will create your own "no pile" for another thrift queen to find. It's honestly so helpful to give yourself that fresh look over your finds to gain a (possibly) new perspective (or to come down from that initial thrift high) before deciding if you ultimately need to purchase.

23. **Ask about returns.** This is a newer tip for postpandemic thrifting, since a lot of spots to shop, and especially ones that have removed fitting rooms entirely, have introduced different return and exchange policies. It's some key knowledge to have on a spur-of-the-moment trip to the thrift where you may not have your measuring tape on hand.

24.

Seriously, just have fun! Don't put too much pressure on yourself to find everything in one trip. This is a strut, not a sprint.

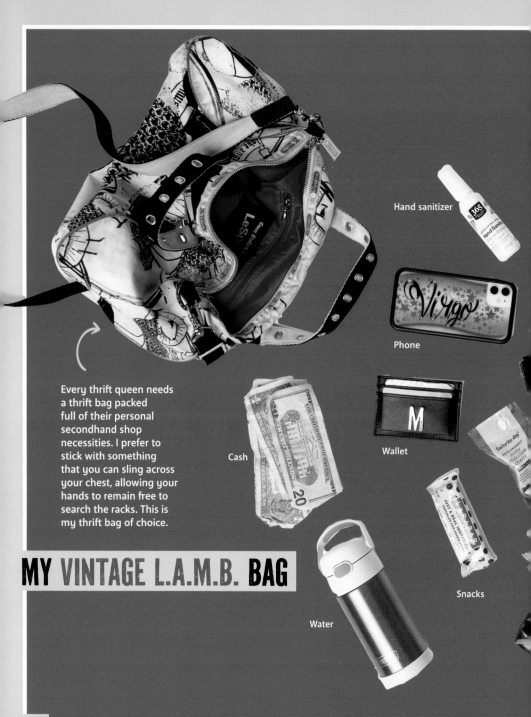

Hand sanitizer

Phone

Cash

Wallet

Snacks

Every thrift queen needs a thrift bag packed full of their personal secondhand shop necessities. I prefer to stick with something that you can sling across your chest, allowing your hands to remain free to search the racks. This is my thrift bag of choice.

MY VINTAGE L.A.M.B. BAG

Water

Headphones
(most thrift stores play a lite FM station or are just plain silent)

Claw clip

Hair ties

Reusable collapsible bag
(to carry your finds home in but also in case they have no carts or none available

Digital camera

Advil

Pack of tissues

Lip balm

Measuring tape

Gloves

Sanitizing wipes

Sunnies

How to "THRIFT MANIFEST" . . . Anything!

Thrift manifesting is an ancient and extremely serious method of secondhand shopping that I've personally been practicing since long before the word *manifest* existed in my vocabulary. This is a superpower most thrifty shoppers may not even know

they possess. But when you aren't simply given access to clothes straight "off the rack," you're forced to play a bit of make-believe. And that "make-believe" mindset, that forced imagination, is where the magic happens.

Okay now, what exactly is thrift manifesting?

Well, it's simply my semi-dramatic way of describing how a piece pulled straight from my dreams can make its way onto the rack at the thrift store right in front of me. Think of it as romanticizing the journey to the find.

Any successful thrift manifest begins with a vision. For example, you see the *perfect* dress for a wedding you'll be attending but the price tag isn't looking so hot. You watch *The Sweetest Thing* for the first time and simply *must* find one of the countless iconic tops Cameron Diaz dons throughout the film. Sometimes, if the piece is that important, yes, I will hold a seance of sorts and offer my firstborn child to the thrift gods in exchange for the goods. But if you are not quite as dramatic as yours truly, you can try this instead . . .

I personally use Pinterest for the majority of my thrift store inspo boards and manifestations, so if you're not familiar with how to use the site's basic functions, I give a more detailed breakdown of my "*pinning*" process in chapter 5. But if you're a Pinterest stan much like myself, let's get our manifest on!

1. **Head to Pinterest and create a board.** (I say turn it to secret mode. This is between you and the thrift gods.) Add the image of the item that sparked this particular manifest need!

2. **Scroll and roll.** Curate a few more images that give a similar vibe as your OG inspo . . . not identical but same silhouette, color, or some other shared detail.

3. **Give yourself time.** In our world of "send me the link!"–focused instant gratification, we lose sight of the time it takes to curate a sustainable wardrobe that is so totally you. Some thrift manifestations take a few days while others can take *years* to come to fruition. Patience is a top thrift virtue and a skill you must always keep in your kit. It will stop you from purchasing something that may be close to what you're looking for but ultimately isn't "the one."

4. **Give that board some love.** Pull that board out often and especially before taking off on any kind of thrift excursion. I've created a bit of a ritual out of it, always sitting down at my laptop for around twenty minutes (you can also look it over on your phone before heading in) and reminding myself what the goal is. Keep the images fresh in your mind along with your hopes and dreams when trying to manifest those bad boys!

5. **Jump outside the box.** Of course, check your go-to thrift spots, but for my queens who tend to stick solely to their local Goodwill, maybe stop by an estate sale or your closest antique mall. You may walk out empty-handed but if you've been putting into practice the steps above, you may just *shimmy* away with that hidden gem you've been waiting for.

6. **Take it to the resale sites!** If you aren't having luck in person, eBay is my go-to and an absolute gold mine for finding the most specific and obscure thrift manifestations.

MACY'S THRIFT MAP OF ATTACK

My rule of thumb when hitting any secondhand shop is moving section by section based on how visible the items are. Bulkier items like shoes, bags, jackets, and furniture are easier to spot upon walking in than, say, the dresses, jeans, and tops stuffed onto the racks.

FIRST STOP: Bags and/or shoes. These first two can be interchangeable depending on your mood and needs or current thrift desires. They are often located near each other and displayed in a way that makes them more visible than the clothing items hanging on the racks. With these items being more readily visible to the eye upon walking into the thrift store, they tend to get picked over the quickest. In other words, if there is a star piece, aka a designer item or really any standout find, it's going to be snagged as soon as someone spots it.

NEXT: I'll do a quick first-take overview of the furniture area, again to look for a standout piece, easy to spot due to size. If I do happen to find a winner for my home that's too large to throw in my cart, I'll probably purchase it on the spot and run it out to my car before continuing on my search. I've just lost far too many home scores by thinking, *Oh, it will still be there when I go to check out.* Sometimes yes, but most times no, so if you love it, don't risk it!

NEXT: To the outerwear! These aren't displayed any differently than the other clothing sections but they are easier to sift through and spot pieces in because of the size and shape of the garments.

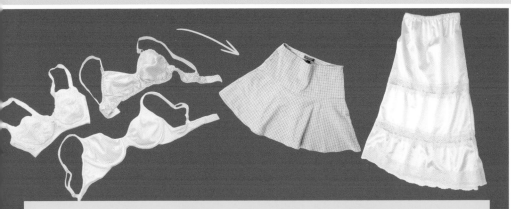

Intimates → Skirts → Dresses → Pants → Jeans → Tops

CHA
3

oTER

The Three E's

I PROMISE WE'LL GET BACK TO FASHION SOON. BUT BEFORE WE CAN GO ANY FURTHER IN YOUR QUEST TO become a thrift icon, it's time for you to let go of whatever icks or preconceived notions you may have about pre-loved pieces. Our world, our wallets, and the lives of others depend on it.

Everyone has "that moment" that catapulted them into the world of secondhand fashion. You grew up thrifting your back-to-school clothes, you're a single mom trying to make ends meet after a deadbeat daddio peaced out, you took a science class and were awoken to climate change being a very real thing, maybe you watched the documentary *True Cost* and were as disgusted as I was by the blatant mistreatment of fast-fashion garment workers, or maybe you've simply realized that you can find designer pieces for discount prices and level up your wardrobe in ways you had only dreamed of before. Regardless of what "it" was, intentional or not, you entered the world of sustainable fashion and (hopefully) decided to give a shit.

The "Three E's"—economics, environment, and ethics—are, in my mind, the key pillars of *sustainability*. They also perfectly describe the road map that I and many others traveled down on our way to becoming secondhand shoppers as well as generally more thoughtful consumers.

A great many of you who picked up this book are probably regular thrifters. But my hope is that the group of you out there who are still a tad skeptical will hear me out on the Three E's, then come back and tell me if that new Zara sweater or Amazon "dupe" is really worth it.

Economics

My first observation as a teen girl who visited the thrift store weekly was the access it afforded people. For decades, the fashion industry has been built on exclusion, creating a class divide based on the types of garments one can afford to purchase. To a certain extent, secondhand shopping beautifully blurs that divide and allows anyone the chance to purchase a pair of Prada kitten heels for $3.99 or the newest pair of Lululemon yoga pants at less than a fifth of the OG price tag.

Now, let's be clear: money and access do not equal style. The most fashionable human beings I have ever had the pleasure of meeting have all come

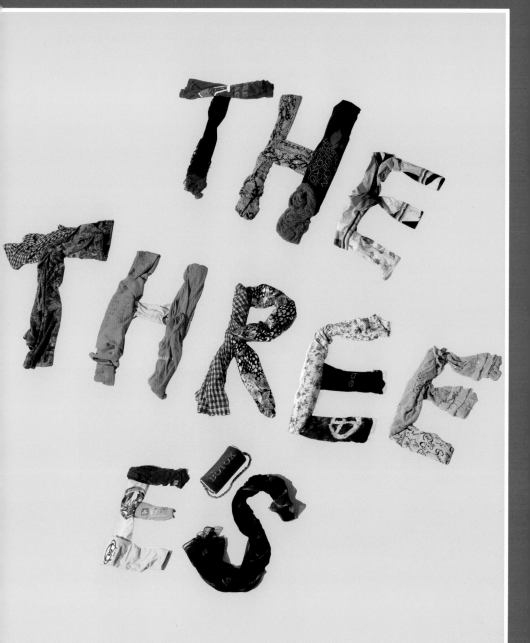

from a similar *DIY*, make-it-work, could-literally-put-on-a-trash-bag-and-stun background. They've been pushed to create what they desire without breaking the bank and that's something we can all learn from (especially those of us who love to buy clothes!).

Yet, even with secondhand shopping being more popular than ever (the US secondhand apparel market grew to $39 billion in 2022 and has been projected to reach $70 billion by the year 2027), heading to the thrift store when you need a "new" pair of jeans or winter coat still isn't the norm, and that needs to change. Our world is the most expensive it's ever been and with most sustainable/ethical brands being out of the average person's clothing budget, not to mention the fact that many of them lack size inclusivity, we have to start prioritizing the reuse of resources that already exist. Secondhand shopping is the answer.

Local thrift stores not only provide space for you to save on your own purchases but they also allow you to pour money back into your own community, as opposed to further filling the pockets of those profiting off the labor of others . . . and the resources of our planet.

Environment

To be real with you, my choice to thrift my entire wardrobe had absolutely nothing to do with the environment. As I mentioned above, I started thrifting because it was cheap and accessible. My teen years were spent so hyperfocused on what I was going through. In my head, at home, and with my body. Me, me, me. I was definitely a bit self-centered, as many teens can be, and it wasn't until college that I was awakened to the urgency of the global climate crisis, discovering that the fashion industry, this untouchable thing I held up high upon a pedestal, was one of the largest contributors.

"The average US consumer throws away 81.5lbs of clothes each year," according to Martina Igini, managing editor of Earth.org. This contributes to the 11.3 million tons (25 *billion* pounds) of textiles being tossed away annually. Now, I know we all know that shit has to go somewhere, and that somewhere isn't into thin air—quite the opposite. Those billions of pounds of Shein this and Boohoo that end up in landfills. As this waste decomposes, methane gas is released into the air. Not so hot, huh?

With so much of our clothing being manufactured by *fast-fashion* brands, defined by Merriam-Webster as "an approach to the design, creation, and marketing of clothing fashions that emphasizes making fashion *trends* quickly and cheaply available to consumers," the materials these tons of garments are being made from are cheap as shit, typically having a short life span in your closet and lasting a true lifetime in the landfill. To keep costs low and output high, these fast-fashion brands frequently turn to synthetic fabrics like polyester, nylon, and spandex. And while these materials are touted for their versatility, they are essentially made up of plastic and can take upwards of two hundred years to decompose. But to so many of us this conversation often ultimately ends in an out-of-sight, out-of-mind mentality. We feel more comfortable only worrying about the here and now, ignoring the fact that every minute we spend not trying to rectify this issue will make it exponentially more difficult to fix in the future, and eventually it will become impossible to fix at all.

Ethics

This is where I officially filed for divorce from fast fashion. To be frank, the second I stopped seeing clothing as "just clothing" and began to consider the human beings who put their blood, sweat, and tears into making it, fast fashion became just about as ugly and foul as Ron DeSantis's politics. The conditions in which a majority of the people making your "super cheap" viral fast-fashion dress are working are horrendous. And guess what? They (most times) aren't making a living wage. You wouldn't want it for your grandpa, your dad, your sister, and you most definitely wouldn't want it for yourself. So why have we normalized being desensitized to the working conditions of those who create the clothes we claim to love so much?

I'm no stranger to the world of fast fashion. I worked at Forever 21 in high school and am convinced we were brainwashed into believing clothing just appeared at the mall in mass quantities and colors. I'm talking about 2010, when fast fashion hadn't quite yet taken the internet by storm. To me, the mid-2000s were the years of the "*mall girls*." We only saw cheap price tags and item after item at our fingertips. We continued to buy, buy, buy, never stopping to consider why the prices were so low or where these garments were actually coming from.

And fast fashion isn't the sole culprit. On average, the fashion industry as a whole profits off underpaid human beings, more specifically women of color, by outsourcing labor to countries where workers can be paid less than a living wage. In past decades these conditions were kept from the public eye under lock and key but with the rise in awareness surrounding the ethics attached to our clothing via social and traditional media, the jig is quite literally up.

No, it shouldn't solely come down to the consumer, but with a majority of brands spouting never-ending excuses about why they can't ensure a living wage for their workers (while the companies continue to mass-produce and rake in billions) and lack of transparency around working conditions, it does fall to us to remove the blinders. We can't claim ignorance any longer.

Now, don't get me wrong. I don't expect everyone to buy everything secondhand. It's not the realistic answer; I get that. I'm not out here screaming "fast fashion for no one!" because when it comes to secondhand scores, there is a lot to be said about size privilege (which we'll chat about in the next chapter) and time privilege. I mean, hell, one of the biggest thrift tips I gave you was "take your time," and not everyone has time. However, I'm looking at those who have created careers off the influence they hold in the virtual fashion world. And those with immense privilege and access. These fast-fashion brands are not thriving solely off the low-income shoppers who turn to them as an economic necessity. Instead, it's the extreme uptick in overconsumption, driven by influential voices in the social media sphere, that keeps this exploitation machine going. Again, let's all permanently remove our blinders because there needs to be a serious shift in the way we see clothing.

What About Thrifting FAST Fashion?

These days it's almost impossible to go thrifting without seeing countless fast-fashion garments stacked on the racks. And I can't lie, I do let out a bit of a bummed-out sigh when I come across what seems to be a score, only to look at the tag and see SHEIN staring me in the face. More frequently, I won't purchase that piece. Truthfully, because I know the quality is pretty crap and it leaves a bad taste in my mouth. However, fast fashion isn't just represented by the exclusively online brands most of us associate with the term. It's H&M, Zara, Urban Outfitters, Victoria's Secret, American Eagle, Hollister, Abercrombie & Fitch, Uniqlo, and countless other labels many of us either grew up wearing or longing to own. Again, these brands also cover the secondhand sphere with their more current styles or vintage pieces. And if someone doesn't give them a second chance, yup, you guessed it . . . they're headed to the landfill.

At the end of the day, it will come down to personal preference, but thrifting fast fashion is not "bad." In fact, if you are newer to this way of shopping and just starting to learn the tricks of the thrift, purchasing your go-to fast-fashion brands from the secondhand market can help aid you in your transition. That way you can still wear the brands you're comfortable in or have grown accustomed to without contributing to the demand for more to be made.

I want to pause here for a moment and have a little shimmy together. I'm honestly just thrilled you're here and grateful to have you on this mission with me! You've either already begun to step away from fast fashion and are here to continue to hone your skills, or you're a first-time thrifter looking to be part of the solution and level up your personal style at the same time. Either way, I'm so excited to be on this journey with you!

CHA

4

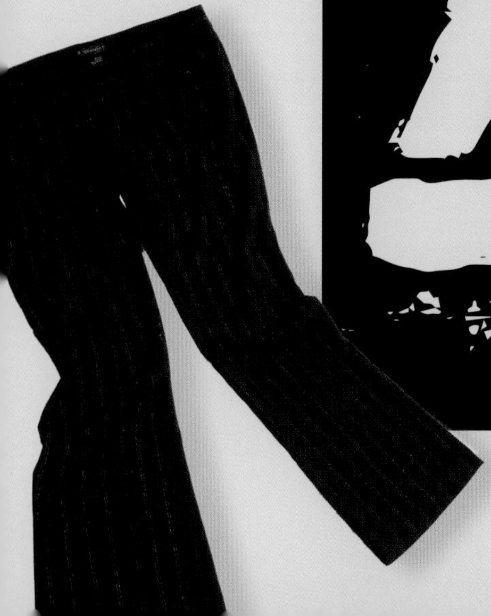

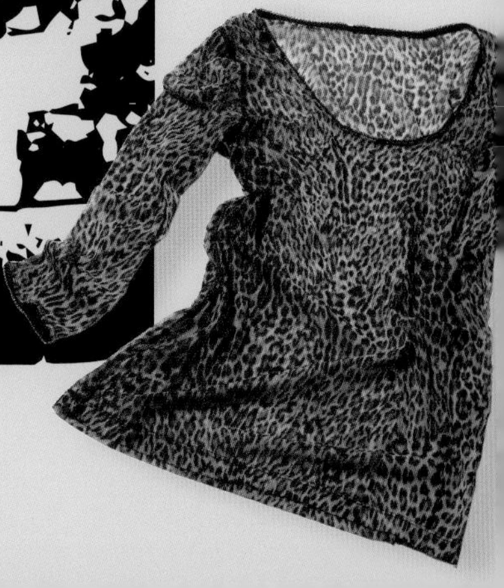

Finding the PERFECT FIT

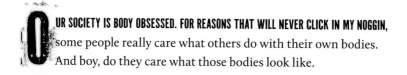

OUR SOCIETY IS BODY OBSESSED. FOR REASONS THAT WILL NEVER CLICK IN MY NOGGIN, some people really care what others do with their own bodies. And boy, do they care what those bodies look like.

Size Inclusivity VS. Fashion and How Secondhand Shopping Plays a Role

The fashion industry has long prioritized thinness. This fact leaves us unable to honestly discuss the ways in which we shop without delving into how our own buying experiences can and do differ based on our size.

I've always been smitten with shopping, more specifically secondhand shopping. You guys know that by now. Diving into the racks, inspiration in hand, endless options at my fingertips. Nevertheless, having this chat with you now, I have to question if part of the reason I love it so much is the unlimited access I have always had to garments, based on my size.

Regardless of that access, I, like many of you reading this, have struggled deeply with my own body acceptance. I've been on the road to recovery from an eating disorder for years now. But for me, that journey has been so much more than *just* repairing my relationship with food. Honestly, the biggest part of my personal recovery thus far has been dismantling the internal fat phobia I had no idea existed inside me. I needed to eliminate the blind spot I had when it came to recognizing *size privilege* and the role it can play when shopping secondhand.

Let Me Tell You a LITTLE Story . . .

It was 2010 and I was headed to the fitting room at a thrift store with my childhood best friend. We loved the same clothes, scoured through the same racks at the same time, yet my cart was full time and time again with countless options while hers held only a piece or two. This I now see as a reflection of my own *thin privilege.*

At the time, I naïvely thought she enjoyed watching me try on piece after piece, calling me her little Barbie because everything "fit" me just right. She'd

help me choose what to bring home and rock to school the next day, or to the club we were going to that night. I would go on about how my body looked in each outfit and she would console me when I complained about my perceived body flaws. Yet I was so blinded by my own thin privilege that I couldn't even see the difference in my own best friend's buying experience and relationship to shopping compared to my own. There came a point, a year or so into my recovery, after actively zipping my own lips and listening to others' lived experiences, that I came to realize how her options were, in fact, more limited than mine, whether we were at the mall or the secondhand shop. Reflecting on it now, I wish I had realized it then, had acknowledged that yeah, there were indeed fewer options for her and that it was indeed absolute bullshit. Having this "aha" moment a decade later is doused in my own privilege and it doesn't help propel this dialogue any further (which is necessary for change) when we can't simply acknowledge these realities. If this hits home and makes you feel embarrassed, or like a crappy friend, feel those emotions because I definitely did. It's okay to learn, look back on the past, and say, "We can really do better. Let's actually do better!"

There can be quite a bit of resistance to the term *thin privilege*. It often puts people on the defensive. "But I'm not even that thin!" "I've struggled with an eating disorder my whole life!" While everyone's experiences with their own body issues and insecurities are completely valid, if you can walk into most mainstream fashion retailers and not have to wonder if the store you've set foot in carries your size, you benefit from thin privilege. We have to acknowledge that more.

It's not about pointing fingers or making people feel bad, but this prioritization of thin bodies is plain as day when you look at the lack of size inclusion throughout most of the fashion industry, and the even fewer options then available to score beyond a size XL on any given secondhand shopping trip.

Thrifting BEYOND a Straight Size

People often leave me comments online stating some version of the sentiment, "It's easy for you to find the good stuff because you are thin," and they're not wrong. It is easier and there are exponentially more options for a body like mine at the thrift store. Lucky for us, a little thing called the World Wide Web has allowed communities to form based on shared interests, therefore introducing me and many others to some fabulous people who know a thing or two about finding their own *perfect fit* at the thrift, and can speak to secondhand shopping from something other than another thin-bodied perspective.

I met my close friend YouTuber Carrie Dayton in 2019. We hit it off instantly, bonding over our borderline obsession with nostalgia and all things used. Naturally, we began thrifting together and I quickly realized her experience exploring the secondhand shops was a bit different from my own.

Carrie, more of a casual secondhand shopper for most of her life, would often thrift props for videos and snag cute clothing for herself here and there. But it wasn't until a few years into her YouTube career, when Carrie felt the urge to start stepping away from fast fashion and began integrating more thrifting into her content, that she really started to see the size disparity. "As it became a larger part of my job, I began thrifting more frequently and started to notice more and more that my YouTube counterparts making similar content, with

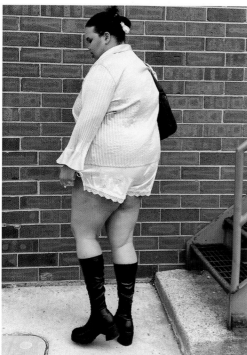

whom I would go thrifting in person or watch hauls they posted online, were finding a lot more stuff than I was. I was scouring the entire thrift store, going through every rack, and was only able to seek out a very small percentage of what they would find."

There are frequent discussions in the sustainability space about how secondhand is always better. Hell, I've absolutely been a part of those conversations—this book is part of that conversation. But as Carrie noted, "Yes, everyone should be shopping secondhand but there is another, more nuanced part of the discussion, that *straight-sized* people can more often glaze over." Carrie herself enters this conversation and opens up about it frequently on her YouTube channel, with acknowledgment of her own size privilege, in the sense that she can (depending on the brand) still fit into items that fall right under the plus-size mark. But what about the women, more than half the US population of women, in fact, who can't? Even current *eco-conscious brands* that are making huge strides in terms of sustainability initiatives are often, as Carrie said, "still throwing crumbs at fat people."

This is not to say that thrifting is only for those of a specific body type. To the contrary, digital fashion creator and model Moe Black felt pulled to start sharing her secondhand finds with the virtual world because of frustration after receiving comments from plus-size viewers who were defending their choice to stick solely to fast fashion based on the lack of options for them at their local thrift stores.

"There are pieces at the thrift for plus-size people and this idea that there is nothing for us just makes more clothing end up in landfills. What we should be doing is opening up the dialogue surrounding these privileges and giving plus-size people tangible tips for shopping secondhand." One of those tips from Moe is "expand your idea of what thrifting means, go to estate sales, flea markets, swap meets, it's not just going to thrift stores."

Additionally, Moe credits the virtual thrift world with being a great spot to continue your secondhand search. "Get creative. These people listing plus-size clothing are typically older and won't be using the same keyword search terms as Gen Z and younger millennial resellers. An item likely won't be listed as a Y2K (frequently used to describe the aesthetics of the late '90s to mid-2000s), sparkly grunge top, so get familiar with the actual cuts and forms of clothing you like and use those as your specific search terms." I can personally attest to this, as some of my best virtual thrift scores have come from what I like to refer to as a "*Poshmark mom.*" This type of seller may have the goods but won't necessarily know how to list the item "keywords"-wise, beyond the actual brand, cut, or fabric of the piece.

Next, I asked Moe for her thrift plan of attack. I gave you queens mine back in chapter 2, but thrifting beyond a straight size isn't my forte, so we are passing the mic to Miss Moe!

1. Have your measurements in your notes app! (This applies to everyone!) Sizing in general is so unreliable and really does fluctuate from brand to brand, especially when we're talking vintage.

2. A lot of thrift stores will have one to three rows of specifically plus-size pieces. Moe suggests hitting those racks first. She'll look for pieces in her size but also items that may be too big or small that she can rework/upcycle back at home.

3. Don't purchase a piece solely because it is your size. Purchase it if you love it and can truly see yourself wearing it.

4. Now, off to the accessories! Shoes and bags are great spots to explore and play with items that you can pair with anything.

5. For tops and sweaters, Moe encourages looking for pieces that may not be "technically" plus-size but have a good amount of stretch to them or are truly just a *vanity size*.

6. Brands to look out for: each time you thrift, take note of the pieces that fit your body best and make you feel good. These will sometimes be brands you truly never thought would be "fashion," but styled with a bit of thought, they can really be a fit. "Cato, Rampage, and Coldwater Creek are a few of my faves. I also love anything vintage Lane Bryant and Zoey and Beth."

Brands and Spots 2 SHOP

Here is a list of plus-size-friendly that my followers (aka digital thrift baddies who know their shit) have suggested you be on the lookout for when thrifting:

BRANDS

A New Day

Torrid

Roaman's

Jessica London

Premier Collection

Definitions

Berkertex

Jaimie Nicole

Zana Di
(superhot jeans)

Notations

Zenobia

Croft & Barrow

White Stag

Ruby Rd.

Eloquii

Baby Phat

Venezia

+ SECONDHAND SPOTS

Plus BKLYN
(consignment store in Brooklyn, New York)

Berriez
(vintage shop in Brooklyn, New York)

Iconic Atomic
(Palm Springs, California,
very plus-size friendly)

Luvsick Plus
(www.luvsickplus.com)

Lost Girls Vintage
(Chicago—carrying a selection
from Luvsick)

Plus Bus
(Los Angeles, California)

Goldies Vtg
(Etsy)

More Than Your Average
(www.morethanyouraverage.com)

I Want Seconds
(Portland, Oregon)

Heavy Duty Vintage
(Etsy)

Nanometer Vintage
(Etsy)

Ethical Bodies
(https://ethicalbodies.com)

Magma Vintage
(vintage shop in Los Angeles, California)

Gender IDENTITY

We have already discussed in great detail how magical a place the thrift can be. But for those yearning to push back on the gender constructs and fake-ass clothing "rules" that have been placed on us since birth, thrifting can serve as a direct path to true self-expression.

Think about when you walk into a typical retail store. You're instantly bombarded with campaign ads of models selected by the brand, mannequins donning the latest line, even employees dressed in that label's garments, all meant to evoke a similar vibe. The store often has a certain image they want to portray, one that is frequently based on their skewed idea of the "ideal body" and societal norms surrounding gender. It is plain to see that there is an expectation of who the clothes are made for.

Think of Abercrombie in the early–mid 2000s, with one side for "girls" and one for "boys," models all of a very specific body type, and seemingly not a thought given to inclusivity. Since that time, many brands have "made changes," introducing a bit more body representation and extending sizing a tad (still not enough!). But the expectations surrounding gendered clothing still seem to ring loud in most traditional retail experiences.

This practice, as you can imagine, creates an exclusionary environment that is nonexistent in the thrift store.

As genderqueer fashion creator Brendan Dunlap explained, "In the thrift it's just about the clothes, the pieces themselves, instead of connecting to the brand's idea of who I 'should' be or who 'should' wear these clothes. It's just me in the space being presented with amazing, one-of-a-kind things and deciding for myself, is this me? Is this something I'm excited to buy or want to try on? Could this dress, even if it wasn't necessarily intended for me upon creation, be something I find fun? And it turns out, YES, the dress was fun and was definitely for me!"

Brendan then excitedly detailed for me the moment he decided to thrift a dress for himself for the very first time. "A denim dress from Buffalo Exchange, that was the first dress I bought. It was cute but I never ended up wearing it. The first dress I purchased and was really excited to wear was during my time studying abroad in Prague. It was from a tiny thrift store. The dress was vintage

with polka dots and when I put it on I felt like an alternate character. I instantly loved how the clothes could make me feel so different, yet so me."

Secondhand shops have the ability to create an environment where anything feels possible for anyone. Mars, a nonbinary fashion enthusiast with a passion for accessible style, grew up in Memphis, Tennessee, where true self-expression was limited. Attending a private Christian K–12 school, "I had a specific uniform I had to wear daily. It was your typical male-and-female, you wear *this* and they wear *that* type of atmosphere. It wasn't till college that I entered the women's section at my local thrift and was truly blown away by what I had been missing this whole time." Mars credits thrifting as an important tool in helping them discover their gender identity. "I just think it's so cool and ultimately really special that something someone else didn't want and tossed away allowed me a new perspective on who I am."

On the other side of the register I spoke with Sin, the owner of Magma Vintage, a vibrant oasis filled with one-of-a-kind vintage and *deadstock* (items that were never sold when created) pieces tucked away in LA's Chinatown, bursting with color and energy.

Sin feels extremely passionate about creating a space that feels inviting, comfortable, and accessible to the LGBTQIA+ community. "I'm nonbinary and a lot of first-timers in the shop who are also nonbinary but may be more masculine-presenting will tell me they've been afraid to explore the feminine side, but when they come to Magma, they feel comfortable enough to step into those pieces and present more feminine without being scared of how they will be perceived.

"Maybe people have seen pieces like the garments we carry and been a little too scared to pick them up [in the traditional shopping world] or never been offered vintage gems in their size. Then they come to a place like Magma where community forms and people are like, yeah, you look really great in that! Building each other up! Especially if you're a different body type or gender, you have that community support, where you feel affirmed. I love seeing people feel good and comfortable. People wearing what *they* like is really beautiful, I feel that. Being totally free, it's what expression is all about."

Magma Vintage, you should know, carries the best selection of plus-size items I have ever seen, especially when it comes to Y2K-specific garments. If they exist, Sin will find them.

FINAL Note

There is no true "sustainability" in living selfishly and without empathy for others. I hope this chapter leaves you feeling seen or with a bit more of an understanding of what others may experience as they navigate their own journeys through self-expression and secondhand shopping.

Whether you start with a "new to you" winter coat, a dress for a party you would have previously tapped a fast-fashion brand to find, or you want to transform your wardrobe completely, the thrift universe is for *you* . . . it's for everyone! Now, speaking of a secondhand wardrobe transformation, that just happens to be my specialty. So let's dive in!

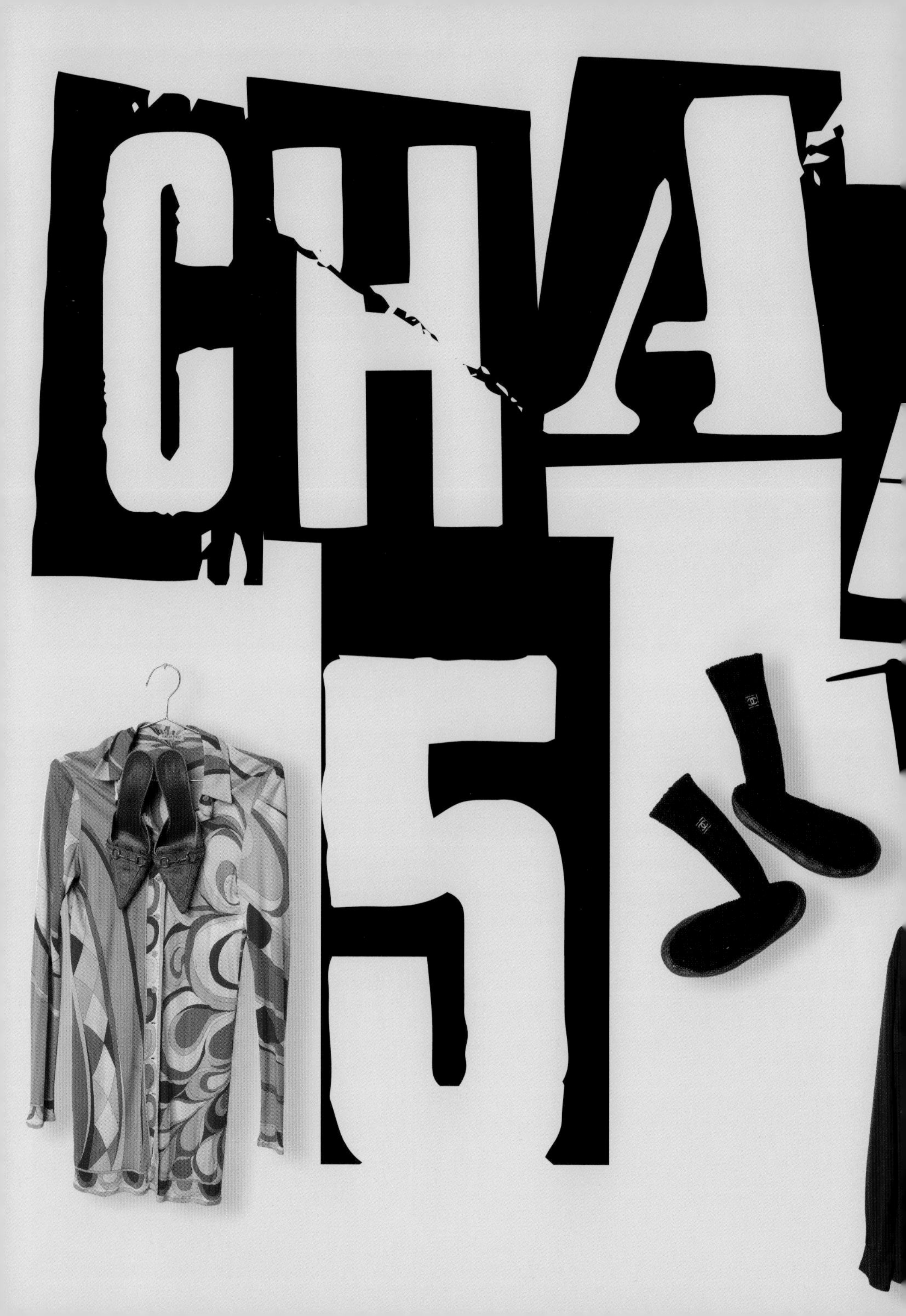
CHA
5

Trash but MAKE IT FASHUN

AS A TEENAGE GIRL, I GOT DRESSED NEARLY EVERY DAY BY PULLING A SECONDHAND SWEATER OVER my head and putting my foot through the leg hole on a three-dollar pair of jeans. It was an attempt to create what I couldn't yet afford. I was deeply envious of my many classmates who could buy whatever was "cool." Half of me knew that the way I shopped was special, but the other half truly longed to blend in with everyone else. The elusive "they" has always been quite successful at convincing us that the wealthiest person in the room is ultimately the chicest, and that access equals style. This chapter is going to bust that myth right down the middle, chew it up, and spit it right back out.

As we learned in chapter 2, the magic lives in the make-believe, and if my time spent shimmying through the world of secondhand shopping has taught me anything, it's that it's extremely possible to look chic as hell in thrifted clothing.

How I CURATED a Fully Thrifted Wardrobe

How do I want to feel? This is the question I ask myself each time I pluck a piece off the rack before giving it a place in my 99.9 percent secondhand wardrobe. I get such a thrill when simply peering around my closet because any piece that meets my eyes tells a tale.

Back in school I was never the best at retaining facts or taking tests, hence my not-so-great grades. However, when it comes to my closet, I can recall exactly where each piece was found, as well as *why* I decided to give it a home. When you hunt for a piece, finding a total treasure among "trash," it provides you with the feeling that *"this* piece was meant for me," an excitement that simply cannot be captured by the standard retail shopping experience.

It's why a wardrobe that leans more to the secondhand side is going to ultimately feel more "you" than that pile of fast fashion

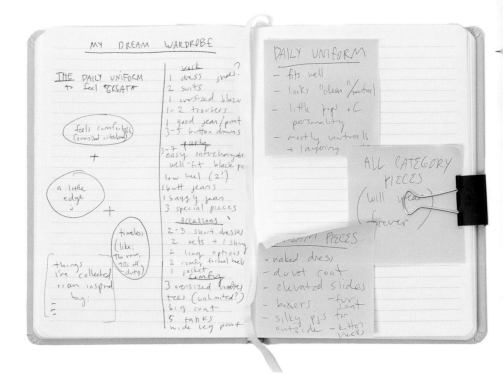

ever did. Dressing for how you want to *feel* as opposed to how you want to *look* to others is the key to using fashion as a form of true self-expression.

Some of you may have the art of the secondhand wardrobe on lock, while others are joining us here as first-time thrifters. Whether you're a pro or not, we can all benefit from taking stock of our closets, seeing first where we can let go, and then filling in the gaps—with fabulous thrift finds, of course!

I want you to grab a piece of paper (notes apps work too) and make a list of the go-to, day-to-day items you simply cannot live without. Think about what you feel good in, your particular lifestyle staples. Do you need a certain number of slacks for the office? Is there a type of shoe necessary for your morning commute? How many vintage bathrobes do you need to do your morning skin care and shimmies? Okay, that last one could just be me, but you see what I'm getting at here.

SECOND CHANCES

Side note: Don't be afraid to add aspirational items here too! This is your personal master list for *your* dream wardrobe. So ask yourself, What pieces have I felt pulled to try out but not been able to find at a traditional retailer? What items have felt unattainable due to price tag or size but I have a feeling I could rock?! Dream big and write down all those future thrift manifestations.

We're building out your most authentically *you* dream wardrobe.

Now take your list into your current closet or clothing storage setup and cross off the items you have, leaving just the pieces you need to fill in the gaps.

Next we are going to put into practice a bit of that thrift manifest insight you gained a few chapters back. This is the really fun part! You're going to use Pinterest or whatever photo collage app tickles your fancy to turn this list into a visual representation of what you want your wardrobe to look and feel like.

1. Go to Pinterest.com and click "your profile." Once there, hit the little addition sign on the right side of the screen. Here you will have three options, to create a pin, idea pin, or board, and you are going to select "create board." I recommend naming it by season, for example, "SPRING/SUMMER WARDROBE (thrift inspo)." Pinterest will then curate some images for you to scroll based on the name of your new board. There may be a few images that resonate with you and the virtual visual wardrobe you're building out but if not simply click "done." Now, let's help you get ahold of that inspo you're after!

2. Grab the list developed above, select whichever category you'd like to start with, and type the item you are looking for into the Pinterest search bar (located at the top of the web page).

3. For example, you can type in keywords as simple as "work slacks" or "casual trousers" and watch photos containing just that roll in, covering your screen. This next step will look a smidge different on a web page versus in the Pinterest app.

- **If curating your board from a desktop or laptop:** Click the little red "save" icon at the top right side of the specific image you would like to add to your board.

- **If curating your board from the Pinterest app on your phone:** Hold down the image with your finger and a toggle of three different icons will appear. Tap the pin icon and you will be transferred to a page listing all boards you have previously created. Here you will click the name of the current board you are working on and that image will automatically be added.

Continue to work your way through the dream wardrobe "master list" you created above, until your board is filled with every item you'll be looking for when hitting the thrift.

4. This next step is what really helps keep me focused and organized when taking off to hunt down these pieces. It's time to go in and organize your board by type of clothing piece or accessory. My preference when doing this is to put shoes at the bottom, followed by bags, then pants, skirts, tops, dresses, and jackets. Last, near the top of the board I recommend adding some fully styled outfits for inspo on how to wear the items you've been pinning (but do whatever works best for you!).

To me, Pinterest almost feels like a thrift shop in itself. You scroll and roll, pulling from whatever aesthetics you desire, then challenging yourself to go find your own version. As Lindsay Lohan's iconic character in *Mean Girls* said, "The limit does not exist!" and that most definitely applies to your secondhand wardrobe. I know it's overwhelming, but look how much you already know! I can just see that thrift queen energy radiating from you, and your closet is about to get *so* good.

With your thrift list in hand, aka your perfectly curated Pinterest board, you're ready to take off on your secondhand search. It's a tad cheesy, I know, but practice really does make perfect and the more often you hit the thrift, the quicker you'll gain a deeper understanding of how to make used pieces work in your wardrobe.

Trends are on a constant recycle and the pressure to "keep up" has made a direct impact on our closets. These trends, micro or not, are seen going viral on social media or popping up season after season on the runway. What gets me is, if trends are being endlessly recycled, why is the norm to purchase them new? Recycling these trends, which have been revived from past decades, and doing it *in* recycled clothing? Now, *that* makes sense. The thrift store will always be your best option for not just buying said trendy piece but doing it in a way that can truly be more sustainable.

For example, suppose a certain clothing item goes viral and everyone just "must" have it. Consumers often click "buy" before first giving thought to how that specific "on trend" item will fit into their personal wardrobe. Instead, I implore you to pause and release that need for instant gratification. Rather than clicking "buy now," take a screenshot of the piece, throw it on your "manifest" board (that we created together back in chapter 2), and start digging!

Furthermore, I challenge you to take a trip over to your go-to retail spot (or site), take notes or actual photos of the new "trendy" pieces they have on the floor, and use them as a reference guide to finding the OG pieces the new versions were likely inspired by for a fraction of the cost.

Hunting Down DESIGNER DUDS

Now, I know the name of this chapter reads "Trash but Make It Fashun," yet it's not only "trash" you'll find on the racks of the thrift. Back in chapter 3, I referenced the thrift store being a place that allows anyone the chance to purchase a "pair of Prada kitten heels for $3.99," and by that I was quite literally referring to a pair of zebra-print Prada babies my little sister scored for me back in our hometown Salvation Army. I will never forget when she called me screaming over her insane score. These are the moments that will literally send a rush of adrenaline throughout

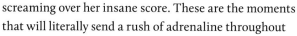

your body. I'm sorry to say it, but the regular retail experience will start to feel extremely dull once this secondhand spark has been ignited.

My nonlinear relationship with designer/ luxury pieces began right back where the majority of my fashion journey did, flipping through magazines as a teen. I'd turn each page, my eyes immediately glancing to the spot in the glossy image where, in teeny-tiny writing, there would be a detailed breakdown of each

item used to create the look . . . along with, of course, how much that item cost. These price points told me that the pieces I desired were far out of my reach, but somewhere down the line the secondhand universe taught me much different.

I spoke with Brit Blanco, co-owner of the insanely popular vintage heaven Treasures of

SOME OF MY FAVE DESIGNER FINDS ♡

I took to my personal wardrobe and pulled out a few of my favorite designer purchases that of course lived a life (or many) before hitting my hot little hands. From the iconic Balenciaga city bag, that I lusted over HARD as a teen, while seeing the Olsen Twins sporting it's slouchy self in 2004. To the vintage John Galliano newspaper dress, which pays homage to one of the most memorable outfits in fashion history... aka the Galliano for Dior look Carrie Bradshaw dawns as she slowly struts through the streets of NYC, in the infamous episode of Sex And The City, "What Goes Around Comes Around". To an extremely special mini Miu Miu bag, a stunning piece from their SS2000 collection, that I never imagined would be mine. These pre-loved pieces all deserved a second chance and I'm honored to have given them just that.

Balenciaga City Bag—Poshmark

Galliano Newspaper dress—Pomchili

Dior shimmy shake top—Seriously Sunday

Gucci bag—The RealReal

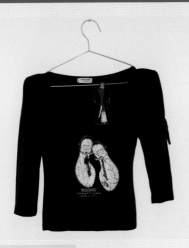

Moschino Top—eBay

Dolce & Gabbana sunnies—The Real Real

Pucci shimmy shake top—a bday gift from my bestie via The Real Real

Gucci heels - Curated Cutie

Donna Karen New York dress—flea market

Miu Miu bag—Voulez Vous Vintage

Chanel slipper socks—Treasures of NYC

NYC, which she runs with her partner, Robert Bird. Thrifters to their core, Brit and Robert are absolute legends when it comes to *dumpster diving* (no, seriously, the first time I met Brit back in 2022 we instantly bonded over our shared love of fishing finds from a literal dumpster if need be) and emerging with one-of-a-kind, sometimes high-end luxury finds. "As soon as Robert and I met we instantly started thrifting and digging through 'garbage' together. When we first moved to New York we would stalk Craigslist to furnish our place and one day we came across a guy selling a 'really nice' (to say the very least) steamer trunk for one hundred dollars." At the time that was quite a lot of cash for the two to drop on a secondhand find for themselves but Brit says, "Robert had a gut feeling it was something really special." The truth is one man's "trash" is some thrift queen out there's treasure. Years went by as the two cherished their Craigslist trunk in their New York City apartment before coming to find out it wasn't just any vintage trunk at all but a Goyard steamer trunk that they scored for just $100. Now, a quick Google search will tell you these trunks are reselling online for anywhere from $5,000 to $30,000, but to Brit and Robert it's priceless. "I couldn't give two shits if it was worth millions. I care about the treasure of it. We keep some of our most sentimental items in that trunk and the piece itself, along with the contents inside, are basically an entire metaphor for our business."

I may sound like a broken record, but I can't help but want to scream from the rooftops how this kind of fashion magic only occurs in the secondhand universe! I fully believe that each and every single one of you has the ability to create your own perfectly YOU personal style, even if you've never felt particularly "stylish" a day in your life. One thing I hope you've learned by now from this book is how BS fashion can be. At the end of the day it's about wearing what makes YOU feel good. Fuck what anyone else says; they can take that up with their own wardrobes. Getting to know these pieces in the thrift store, designer or not, trendy or timeless, will leave you more excited about clothing than ever before.

Plus, I can't stress enough how fun it is to be able to tell everyone how you snagged your vintage Dior blazer at Goodwill for a few bucks, or the same top they bought retail for half the price on Poshmark. It truly never gets old to exclaim, "Thanks, I thrifted it!"

SECOND CHANCES

CHA
6
No Paparazzi

Wardrobe MAINTENANCE

Okay, but WHERE Do I Put It All?

SO, YOU'VE SUCCESSFULLY THRIFT MANIFESTED, MAYBE A LITTLE TOO HARD? NO JUDGMENT HERE, queen. I get it, I feel you, I see you . . . I AM you. However, luckily for you, I've got well over a decade of knowledge about how to keep a wardrobe circular, meaning I try to stay very aware of what is going in and out of my closet, being thoughtful about where my pieces end up when they inevitably leave my possession. I'm frequently asked about storing all the fabulous thrift finds I share with my internet friends daily. Some people assume I must be living inside an episode of *Hoarders*, but I can assure you that my very Virgo self prefers my chaos to be organized.

By no means am I a minimalist. I think people tend to get that concept confused with being passionate about eco-conscious fashion. I like stuff. I really like stuff! In fact, as I sit here chatting with you, I'm at my desk in my wardrobe room surrounded by racks of clothing, shoes, bags, magazines, and a furry cheetah phone that sadly does not work but makes me smile each time I look at it. It's *"organized" chaos* and I wouldn't have it any other way. But there is a method to the madness.

I ❤ ME

You know that big closet cleanout? The one where you're in your pjs, digging out crusty-ass hoodies you've had since college and sorting through jeans that are too big or small. It can be daunting. Personally, I do a few of those big daddies a year. Now, I'm not an expert on organizing. I do what works for me and you do what works for you and your space. What I can help you with is how to keep your closet moving and grooving in a more thoughtful way.

1. **Pull out *everything*** . . . yes, even the pile that has been collecting dust in the innermost corner of your closet. Actually, especially those items.

2. **Time to curate your piles.** We've all heard the classic "keep/toss" but let's broaden those a bit:

A. **KEEP**—these are the pieces you wear like a damn uniform and truly do picture yourself plugging into outfits on a consistent basis.

B. **ARCHIVE**—this is a special category for you guys, my thrift queens. These are the "one-day" and "someday" items. Will you wear them often? No, but do they make you smile and feel happy just knowing they're there, "just in case"? Absolutely yes. I allow myself just a few of what I call my *"archive"* pieces (a word most frequently used to describe clothes from high-end designers' early collections, but it can really be anything that feels special and aspirational to you) that my soul cannot bear to part with or that I want my future child to rock one day. Be picky here, because if not, you'll end up back where you started.

A PEEK INTO Macy's Archive

Found at Out of the Closet in 2019 and what can I say, I fucking love disco!

I will never forget finding this Jordache vintage faux fur at a Salvation Army because one, it's just fabulous, and TWO, the second I pulled it from the rack a group of ladies my mom's age said it was perfect for me and I absolutely HAD to have it, so I obvi listened to them!

Scored at Magma Vintage and will NEVER part with; sorry, babes, no brand tag in this one or I promise I would share!

I personally keep these "archive" pieces in a separate coat closet in my apartment, so they don't overwhelm my daily dressing. But again, you do YOU!

A top passed down to me after my angel bestie grandpa passed away. The most special piece I will ever own.

Snagged at Savers thrift store and is the ultimate hot leather staple. I mistakenly tried to sell it at a closet sale a few years back and luckily the thrift gods stepped in and no one purchased . . . meant to stay mine forever!

The perfect Y2K baby tee . . . that is all.

Akrs skirt, I yanked from a Beverly Hills estate sale for pennies!! Such a hot little unique piece that I wore to NYFW a few seasons ago.

The very FIRST designer bag I ever thrifted . . . probably around 2010 and Marc by Marc Jacobs obvi!

C. DONATE—be honest with yourself about that tie-dye sweatsuit you bought at the peak of the pandemic. Have you touched it since? If not, toss it in the pile! I know it's not the most fun, but this is an opportunity to try on the items that

may not fit anymore and add them to that donation pile as well. Remember, we aren't made to fit clothes; clothes are made to fit us. I heard different variations of this phrase a few years into my own eating disorder recovery and it's been a simple yet guiding light for me as I navigate my wardrobe. If the pants don't fit, pull them out, pass them on, and thrift another pair. The focus certainly does not need to be on shrinking ourselves back into clothes we once wore.

D. CONSIGN—this is where you can turn clothes into cash or . . . even more clothes. Places like Buffalo Exchange, Plato's Closet (you guys already know, a personal fave of mine throughout my teen years!), Crossroads Trading, etc., are all secondhand shopping spots that will sift through your gently worn items and take certain pieces in exchange for store credit or cold, hard cash.

-HOT TIP-

FOR CONSIGNING AT THESE SPACES:

Call the store ahead and ask what they're looking to buy right now. Remember, locations will have different buying needs based on the season or demographic that most frequently shops that spot. Make the call, and if there are items in your donation pile that fit the bill, throw them in a bag, take them in, and see how much you can make!

E. REPAIR—more on the "how-tos" of clothing repairs later in this chapter, but let us not forget that cobblers, seamstresses, dry cleaners, and sewing machines do exist and help extend the life span of our items well past a little stain or snag.

3. **It's time to sort through those donations.** Where are we taking them? Is there a "right" way to donate clothes? Yes and no. I know a lot of us grew up under the guidance that the best thing to do after a closet refresh is take those bags, filled to the brim, and drop them off at the closest thrift store. I'm not saying this is wrong or bad. It's absolutely fabulous and 100 percent better than letting those pieces collect dust in your closet or go into a landfill. But you do have some options here. I typically divide my "donation" pile into three separate categories: store, shelter, and swap.

Like I said, dropping your used goods off at the thrift store is great. But with only a small percentage of the clothing at thrift stores actually being sold, there is a way to keep things a bit more actively circular.

SHELTER DONATION

In the years following the pandemic, the US has been experiencing a serious housing crisis. "There are nearly 600,000 people experiencing homelessness on any given night," according to a 2022 report from the US Department of Housing and Urban Development. With just a simple phone call or quick Google search, the clothing you're letting go of could be put to immediate use at a shelter in your area. All people deserve access to quality clothing and comfort, especially as they navigate being at a place in life where so many treat them as less than. Does it take a bit more time? A bit, but it ensures those pieces will go on to live at least one more life, with a person who truly needs them.

CLOSET SWAP

In the secondhand universe, clothes are not disposable. Garments are meant to be worn again and again and again, then repaired and worn yet again. Hence I live for a good closet swap. I grew up with a single mom and sister and so hand-me-downs were the norm, but it's something I feel we lose touch with as we get older. What's better than a party with free clothes? Get your friends together, have everyone bring a bag or a few pieces, turn on your favorite bops, and shop each other's closets!

Remember the old saying, "Sharing is caring."

REPAIR and REPEAT

Time to talk about repairs, as I think it's safe to say most of us have lost sight of the true potential life span of a garment. We see a few holes, we toss the top. Our shoes give in a bit, so we purchase a new pair. We pass up a perfectly good pair of pants with a stain or stunning suede coat from the seventies simply because we have no clue how to get it clean. Never again!

The THRIFT QUEEN Laundry Routine

Developing a solid laundry routine, one that suits your lifestyle and you'll actually put into practice (time and time again), is just as important as knowing how to navigate the thrift store itself. In order to grant a piece new life, we must be able to care for it after it hits our home.

I bring my items home, steam them → check the tags on the garments (if visible) and separate dry-clean-only items → separate whites and darks → wash on cold → dry on hot

If you found your items at the bins or, say, a yard sale, where everything is sitting in a pile outside, consider a little prewash moment. I usually soak my finds in Lysol Laundry Sanitizer before beginning my thrift queen laundry routine.

What About DELICATES?

I find some of my best secondhand scores in the lingerie/intimates section of the thrift and these pieces (especially if vintage, old, and fabulous) deserve a little extra care. Make sure to have a mesh delicates bag, which can be found at any general store or online and will help protect these pieces during the wash-and-dry process. However, for extra care I do recommend you remove the delicate items from the bag and hang to dry if possible.

Then There Are STAINS . . .

One thing you will without a doubt run into in the secondhand shopping universe is stains. I know this can be the "ickier" side of the thrifting coin to some but it's really not as bad as you think, I promise. As you're flipping through the racks, you'll inevitably pluck out a piece, so psyched over what you've found, only to realize there is a pretty questionable stain staring back at you. This pesky stain may cause most to let out a sigh and put it back, but not YOU! You are a thrift queen and thrift queens know how to work out a stain to sustain new life in a piece. On that front, being able to decipher a stain that is beyond being lifted versus one that is totally removable is a skill you are going to want tucked away in your thrift bag. You'll learn best by trial and error but I do have a few tips and products that help me bring my items back to life. If your "new"-to-you item has a stain, consider the following before applying the laundry routine above.

STAIN REMOVAL

WHAT EVEN IS THIS?!

THERE ARE FOUR TYPES OF STAINS: protein based (animals), tannin (beer, wine, coffee), oil (plant, animal, auto), and dye (ink, grass, mustard, turmeric). Try to determine the stain type, but if it's a mystery (as many from the secondhand world are), turn to one of these two products I use:

OxiClean Versatile Stain Remover (for soaking)

Grandma's Secret Spot Remover (for on the go, also more laundromat friendly)

To Dry-Clean or Try to Clean? That Is the QUESTION!

Most of your secondhand scores will go right in the washing machine at home. However, if you come across, say, a show-stopping vintage coat, the perfect pair of leather pants, or a delicate designer top, you may find yourself asking, How do I get this thing cleaned? Is it worth taking to the dry cleaner? A fair enough question, considering trips to the dry cleaner can add up, and being that one of the most attractive perks of thrifting is how damn cheap it is.

So the question remains, when are we running to the dry cleaner?

The answer is, it depends! I can't lie: with the amount of thrifting I do, I'm a pretty lax dry-clean girl and will try my best to soak, spray, and shine most everything out myself. If you're like me and going to the dry cleaner feels overwhelming or inaccessible, try Woolite 20 Minute Dry Care Cleaner. It's a lifesaver, removing odors and stains and releasing wrinkles. According to the box, it's safe on acetate, cashmere, cotton, linen, ramie, synthetics, wool, silk, and rayon.

SECOND CHANCES

Lay down your leather find.

Mix a few teaspoons of simple dish soap with warm water.

Soak a sponge or cloth in the concoction.

Use dabbing motions to remove dirt without damaging the leather.

(Do not drench the piece, this is not a splash fest, use as little water as possible.)

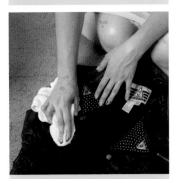

Follow up with a clean, dry cloth, wiping the leather piece down in a sweeping motion.

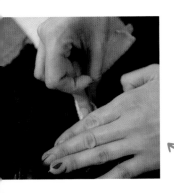

Clean the inside of the garment by turning it inside out and repeating the process (paying closer attention to the points on the garment that touch sweat most frequently, such as armpits, collar, crotch, etc.)

Hang to dry.

You also have the option of purchasing a leather cleaner instead of using dish soap. It may be a bit unconventional but I'll often use the same leather care wipes I take to my car seats on my leather thrift finds—does the trick if you're in a pinch!

CLEANING FUR

Used fur is a tough one but I have cleaned up a few without the help of a dry cleaner and I'll usually do as follows:

Shake out the item (usually a coat).

Use any fur brush (yes, even one you would use on your pet) . . .

. . . and comb the fur in the direction in which the fur lies.

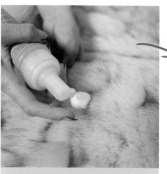

There are various at-home fur cleaners in spray form on the market. I snagged Lana's 3-in-1 Fur Cleaner after seeing it on YouTube a few years back.

Hang to dry.

GOT PILLING? NO PROBLEM!

Another good thing to have on hand is a sweater shaver to remove pilling.

All this being said, if you personally feel better taking an item to a professional or have come across something so special it deserves the star treatment, a dry cleaner can get the job done.

BEFORE YOU HEAD OFF TO THE
DRY CLEANER

- Check every pocket on the pieces you would like to take to be dry-cleaned and remove any tissues, receipts, etc., that could be still sitting in your thrift find.

- If it's an item with specific stains, make note by placing a piece of tape or small pin in any area that may need extra attention. Also, be sure to point out the affected areas on the garment(s) when you call ahead or bring them in to be cleaned.
NOTE: if it is a piece you stained yourself after purchase, give the dry cleaner as much information as possible on how the stain came to be, so they can use best practices to remove it.

- How soon do you need it cleaned? Turnarounds can vary from place to place but I know that the spot I do frequent has to send certain items, for example real vintage fur, out to another facility to be cleaned, adding to the time it can take my items to be ready for pickup. The last few things I personally took in were a faux fur coat, two vintage fur jackets, and a leather bomber. They had the faux fur and leather ready in four days, while the real fur jackets took an extra week on top of that, since they had to be sent out, cleaned, and returned.

How Do I Find the RIGHT Dry Cleaner?

I found my go-to spot, Mr. Dryclean in Sherman Oaks, California, by doing a quick Google search. After taking a thoughtful look through the reviews, I was able to weed out the ones that didn't seem to be a good fit, along with spots that others maybe didn't have the best experience with. Narrowing them down to around three places, I called each up to ask about the specific garments I needed cleaned and compared what they had to say. This is where I recommend letting them know what you would be bringing in, as well as if there are stains versus if you simply just need a fresh cleaning. Inquire about their normal turnaround time on a ticket like yours and about how much it will cost, so there are no surprises when you stop in.

TAILOR Made

We talked about "finding the perfect fit" at the thrift back in chapter 4, but with the help of a *tailor* or seamstress, your search can definitely be simplified. I thrifted my senior prom dress at my favorite Salvation Army back in 2011 and knew right away it was the one. The only problem was that the white one-shoulder beauty was a bit too big and quite a few inches longer than my eighteen-year-old self desired. I wanted to show some leg and the local tailor was able to take my nineties find and create my Y2K teenage dream ensemble. We'll discuss the beauty of upcycling in a bit, but for now, remember the tailor exists and can truly help to enhance the role that piece can and will play in your wardrobe.

When searching for a true garment shapeshifter, it's important to do a bit of research, since tailors have different areas of expertise. It's also beneficial for them to know exactly what you are looking for in this experience. There might be someone in your area who can do it all or you may have to take different projects to different people. Again, Google and the reviews are going to be your best friend. Once you land on a tailor to try, give them a call ahead to see if an appointment is needed. Again, ask about pricing and turnaround time for your item/items. I can't stress this enough: overcommunicate your needs.

Cobblers

One of my most rooted childhood memories involves my grandpa and his shoes. My mother's father, who was my absolute bestie growing up, rarely bought a new pair. Raised in the 1930s by a widowed father of three in Youngstown, Ohio, he walked through the snow to school, to work at the local candy shop, to play with his friends, all in the same pair of shoes. He carried that practice with him as he got older, and anytime the sole gave out or leather was worn in, he would call up his *cobbler*, drop them off for a "facelift," and extend their life span. I honestly remember thinking it was quite weird when I was a little girl. I'd ask my mom, "Why doesn't Grandpa just buy new shoes?" Unbeknownst to me, he was simply being a sustainable king.

It wasn't until I was a bit older and began thrifting shoes I loved and *had* to save from the grave that I understood the true beauty of the cobbler. It's an added expense, yes, but when you can purchase a pair of vintage Gucci slingbacks for $5 and spend $30–$50 to get them ready to wear, it is so incredibly worth it. A good shoe repairperson can help with anything from scuffs and scratches to holes, soles, zippers, and heel replacements.

My grandpa taught me early on that buying new was almost never the answer and to repair whenever possible.

QUESTIONS **TO ASK YOUR COBBLER**

What types of shoes do you specialize in repairing? This will give you an idea of what they do best and what they may or may not be the right fit for fixing.

Do you have any examples of past work? Some will have photos or books presenting their previous makes and mends. This could serve as a good visual representation of the kind of work you can expect from that specific cobbler.

What is your typical pricing for a repair like this? Call ahead to inquire about the services you need and how much that will cost, as it varies from place to place.

What is the average turnaround time for this type of repair? This is especially important if you need the shoes for a specific outing, event, or celebration. Make sure to give them enough time in advance to get those babies looking fab for you!

Now let's get into what we can do if a garment is perhaps unsalvageable as is. This is known as the old *thrift and flip*.

CHA

7

Thrift
AND FLIP

OVER THE NEXT FEW PAGES, I'M GOING TO NEED YOU TO REALLY TAP INTO THAT MAGIC IN THE make-believe mindset as we dive deep into the never-ending world of thrift flips, resellers, and virtual secondhand shopping. After shopping traditional retail most of your life, it's only normal to be accustomed to being presented with a plethora of "cute" options, strategically marketed to you right there in the store as *ready to wear*. While such options do exist in this thrifty land (we'll get to resellers and how to navigate the glorious world of online thrifting a bit later in this chapter), I'm here to retrain your shopper's eye and broaden your mind to see the possibilities in items you would usually never have given a second look. Think digging through piles in a stranger's backyard and fishing out a "rag" that becomes your favorite top, grabbing a torn-up nightgown at Goodwill and cutting it into the perfect cocktail dress. Seeing an item for what it can be versus what it looks like hanging on the rack in front of you.

Seeing an Item for What It CAN Be

The year is 2010, and studs and acid wash are all the rage. This was my first serious thrift-and-flip phase. That year it felt like every "it girl" from the pages of *Teen Vogue* to Tumblr had this very specific pair of denim shorts. High-waisted, frayed edges purposely tattered to bits, and most importantly, the back pockets were covered in silver studs. Needless to say, I desperately had to get my hands on a pair, but with even the most "affordable options" being out of my price range the only choice was to create my own. I vividly remember how empowered I felt to create what I desired with what was accessible to me. I hit my local Salvation Army, headed straight for the jeans, and started grabbing any pair that looked my size with a little room to spare. I was also particularly focused on snagging pairs that had some kind of staining or rips down the legs. I knew these were the items most shoppers would leave behind because of their "imperfections." Where some saw a dirty pair of jeans beyond repair, I saw a new (to me) trendy pair of shorts ready to be shot for *Seventeen* magazine.

Throwing the jeans in my cart, I zoomed to the checkout, eager to rush home and get to chopping! You could and still can buy a plethora of studs, spikes, patches, truly anything to DIY your thrift find, on websites like Etsy or at your local craft store. I had purchased a massive pack of studs, and a few accidental finger pricks later, I was able to bring my vision to life. From that moment on I was constantly reworking my secondhand pieces. But full disclosure: I am by no means a whiz with a sewing machine. You do not need to be a master seamstress to slay a few classic thrift flips. Here are a few no-sew flips I like to rock from time to time!

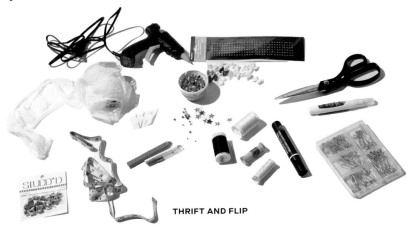

THRIFT AND FLIP

THE SCARF TOP (FOUR WAYS)

SECOND CHANCES

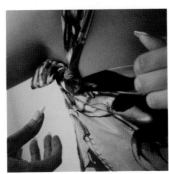
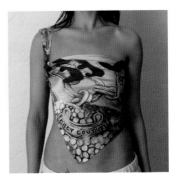

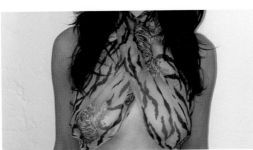

SECOND CHANCES

Not keen on doing it yourself? Not a problem. There are people who have dedicated their days to scouring bins, boxes, and backyards to bring you upcycled garments, as well as their own thrift store scores.

The EVOLUTION and ELEVATION of Resellers

In recent years there has been a bit of misguided discourse surrounding *resellers* and the space they hold in the sustainable-style world. The internet has, without a doubt, lent this marketplace more visibility. However, the practice of reselling has been around for decades upon decades upon literal centuries. From the 1870s onward, flea markets were the go-to spot for resellers to share their goods with the public. But then the 1990s hit and *virtual thrifting* entered the scene, changing the game forever.

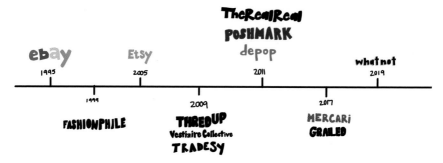

If thrifting in the actual store feels like the Wild West to you, then I imagine the never-ending listings of the digital thrift world may also feel quite intimidating. But again, you know I got you. I've spent my fair share of time getting well acquainted with the virtual thrift landscape, especially during the first Covid lockdown, so let's turn you into a pro too. Warning: you *will* become addicted to the hunt and your browser tabs may never look the same again.

Sifting and Thrifting the VIRTUAL World

- Ask yourself, what am I looking for? Much like the physical thrift universe, you've got quite a few options here. Searching for a specific designer? The RealReal, Vestiaire Collective, Fashionphile, and eBay have you covered. Looking for a few pieces evoking a specific aesthetic or decade? Depop and Etsy boast *millions* of carefully curated shops.

Craving a more adventurous dig, à la the classic thrift store? Poshmark, ThredUp, Mercari, and, again, eBay all have never-ending listings for anything and everything your heart may desire.

- First, have a little peep through your closet. Take note of the styles, fabrics, silhouettes, and brands you like to wear. This will provide you with a good jumping-off point for your online search. Current brands you love and have bought at retail will often have past pieces of a similar vibe just waiting for you to search them up and save them from the grave.

- Next, it's time to start searching. If you've already made your decision based on the above tip of where you want to shop, that's fab. Head there! But if you aren't yet sure which site is best for your quest, utilize Google instead of heading to a specific resale site. Hit the Google search bar (flip to the "Shopping" tab) and type in variations of the kind of piece you're after, decade you're into, designer you like, etc. I like to throw "used" over "vintage" in front of the piece I'm searching up. It's not a foolproof method but I've found it brings the cheaper listings to the forefront. Some of my most frequent searches are "used Y2K tank top," "used sneaker heels," "used DKNY sweater" . . . you get the picture.

- Once you inevitably discover an item you dig, click over to that seller's shop/page to see if they have previously listed anything similar. Chances are, if they have one item you like, they probably have another, but you'll never know unless you look.

- Now that your hunt has begun, I have a few tips to keep in mind and/or cross off your virtual thrift checklist before hitting that "buy" button!

- Before buying *anything*, go on a *like spree*. This is the first thing I do when logging onto any resale site. In short, this involves hitting that little heart icon or double-tapping the listing. 👍🤍

- **Reason #1:** It's essential in helping to curate your wish list of wants. Think of this as your thrift store "cart" but in the online world. Pile in your potential purchases, both to sort through later and to keep your eye on when your picks reduce in price. This practice really helps you out when flipping through multiple sites at once, comparing prices, conditions, etc.

- **Reason #2:** Quite a few secondhand shopping platforms are offer based, meaning prices are nearly never firm. That "like" alerts the seller to your interest, which can frequently lead to them then sending you an offer/discount on their piece. One of my favorite late-night pastimes is searching up a designer that's been on my mind, setting the price toggle from lowest to highest, going on a mega like spree (specifically on Poshmark or eBay), then waking up to offers upon offers the next morning.

- A little note on navigating offers. Most of these platforms will have an offer guide of sorts, which will pop up as you hit "make offer." This can help estimate an amount that works for you but also is one the seller is likely to accept. However, this isn't always on point and there may be an even better deal to be had. Pay attention to how long the item has been up for (there will be a date, usually in small print on the listing) and base your offer off that timeline. For example, if a bag has been listed for three months the seller is probably itching to move it out of their closet or inventory and will probably accept a much lower offer than if the item has only been up for three days.

- Peep the seller's page to make sure they have been active over the past few weeks/months. This will help to ensure the listing is active and that the seller will be communicative in a timely manner.

- Always check the reviews. The top may be cute and the jeans may be fabulous but if the seller's reviews reflect they have a tendency to ghost on shipping, not disclose damage to an item, etc., then it might not be worth your coin.

- Don't be shy about requesting measurements (if not already provided) or any other information you may want to know about the piece you're looking to purchase. However, do be reasonable here. Sellers will, of course, want to help out and share what they can but not all items will have an OG tag or be in "perfect" condition. Remember, we're talking about used stuff, and sometimes the wear and tear will reflect that.

- If buying multiple items from one seller, request bundled shipping. Most will give you a bit of a deal for purchasing more than one item from their shop.

Of course, there is a conversation to be had on shipping and how the packaging of the parcels, sent to you via a virtual secondhand platform, impacts sustainability. Like most everything we've discussed in this book, there is no perfect answer on packaging, but there are steps that can be made to create less waste. I've personally noticed an uptick in sellers shifting to more eco-conscious packaging materials or straight up just recycling shipping containers (boxes, mailers, etc.) to use for their sold items. I find this particularly true when shopping from more person-to-person platforms (Whatnot, Poshmark, eBay, Depop, etc.). The next step is then on us as consumers to be conscious of where the packaging goes, once we have unboxed our goodies. I use a lot of the packaging I receive when gifting to others. Reuse and recycle what you can!

Remember, you're on a quest to become a more sustainable and ethical shopper. Keep this in mind when wondering why a secondhand seller has priced an item for higher than they may have found it at the thrift store. We don't blink an eye at a forty-dollar skirt from Zara but then turn and question the same price on something secondhand. These pieces are most times being curated, cleaned, photographed, posted, marketed, and shipped by one person (or a very small team) and the price reflects all those efforts.

So far we've touched mainly on clothing and accessories, and not home décor. That's intentional, since it can be tough (but not impossible!) to shop secondhand furniture in the virtual world. I tend to rely more on estate sales and Facebook Marketplace (which we're getting into in the next chapter) for my home scores. This is mainly because the shipping of these large goods can run a high price tag.

The FUTURE of Flips

With the market forever evolving, the future of virtual secondhand combines an old format with a modern, community-driven twist.

Platforms like Whatnot are changing the space, adding an around-the-clock live auction-based element to the virtual thrift landscape. When I was introduced to the platform in 2022, I was totally sucked in by how they were fostering a community in ways I'd never seen in this specific sector of the secondhand market. Their platform is a marketplace meets live auction, where sellers can utilize a livestream video function similar to Instagram or TikTok but with the added component of selling their secondhand finds directly to those watching.

Whatnot launched in 2019 with a focus on Funko Pops and other collectibles, but has since seen fashion rise as its fastest-growing category. It allows for a deeper peek into the process of your favorite secondhand seller, as well as a better look at the items themselves. Instead of just static photos on the listing, you the buyer get to see items up close and interact with the seller in real time. Over the past year a few of the secondhand selling platforms mentioned in this chapter have introduced their own live selling features. It feels like a throwback to QVC and the Home Shopping Network (the two merged in 2017) but for items that already exist, and that, to me, is extremely hot and fabulous.

Speaking with Liz Goodno, Whatnot's director of communications, only reaffirmed the inkling I had upon first using it, which was that they really had something special. I saw the excitement both in the sellers and buyers when interacting in this live video format, unparalleled to that of the way virtual secondhand shopping has been presented in the past. "This is the future of resale," Liz told me. "And while our sellers have historically focused on collectibles, they're now moving into fashion. Our goal is to expand into every category and every demographic." Think houses, cars, furniture, etc. Liz exclaims, "The sky's the limit!

@ccspieces Whatnot set up!

Shopping the Flea with EASE

As hot, fabulous, and accessible as virtual thrifting is, truly nothing beats falling in love with a piece IRL *and* getting to meet the person who gave it new life. If I am ever in a new state or city with some time to spare, of course I'll look up the closest thrift store—duh—but I'll also always try to hit up the nearest flea market. Here in LA, every weekend feels like there is a different market on every block. There are truly endless options and incredible vendors but flea markets are everywhere and I promise you have no idea how much creativity is being fostered and brought to life in your own town until you go wander around your local flea market.

TIPS FOR FLEA MARKET SHOPPING

- Get familiar with the layout of your local flea market. Most markets have maps online and accounts across social media to help you navigate their vendor layout.

- Bring cash and a budget for what you want to spend. It is far too easy to go over budget at a flea market, especially when most vendors accept forms of digital payment. Take the amount you want and don't go over! (Truth spill: I break this rule far too often, so be better than me!)

- Have a plan for what you are looking for because it can get overwhelming. Booths are carefully curated with some of the craziest vintage pieces you've ever seen, so it helps to put together a little list for your hunt and stick to it . . . if you can!

- Don't let flea market prices scare you off. Most people are there to sell as much as they can that day and want to at least get their money's worth for their paid spot at the market. Barter, bundle, be kind, be respectful, and have a blast!

- Bring a tote, cart, or wagon to carry your purchases. You may be walking around the market for a while and you don't want to be stuck carrying around a lamp you found at the first booth you visited all day while searching through racks of clothes.

- Along with the above, have a plan for how you will get something home if you are after a large piece. Borrow a large enough vehicle from a friend if need be or rent something like a U-Haul.

- Be friendly! By now you know this is what I deem the most important tool to have when navigating the secondhand shopping world but I think it's especially important at a flea market. Unlike a thrift store or the virtual resale world, you are entering a vendor's space, sifting through their personal curation/collection, and making the purchase directly from them. This thrifty universe is all about relationships and connections, so it's never a bad idea to create a good vibe and rapport with those who hold the keys to the finds!

When it comes to the where, I of course say check your backyard first, starting with your town's closest market, because (and I'll say it till I'm blue in the face!) the small towns really do hit big. However, if you find yourself on a little vacay or want to road-trip to somewhere a bit bigger with a broader selection, I've rounded up a list of markets to know about as a thrift queen on the go!

THE 15 BEST
FLEA MARKETS IN THE US

1. Awesome Flea Market (Shepherdsville, KY)
2. Boulevard Flea Market (New Haven, CT)
3. Brooklyn Flea Market (Brooklyn, NY)
4. Chelsea Flea Market (New York, NY)
5. First Monday Canton (Canton, TX; biggest in the US)
6. Lincoln Road Flea Market (Miami, FL)
7. Mile High Flea Market (Henderson, CO)
8. PCC Flea Market (Pasadena, CA)
9. Portland Flea and Food (Portland, OR)
10. Raleigh Flea Market (Raleigh, NC)
11. Randolph Street Market (Chicago, IL)
12. Rose Bowl Flea Market (Pasadena, CA)
13. Scott Antique Market (Atlanta, GA)
14. Shipshewana Flea Market (Shipshewana, IN)
15. Springfield Antique Show and Flea Market (Springfield, OH)

What's in My FLEA FANNY

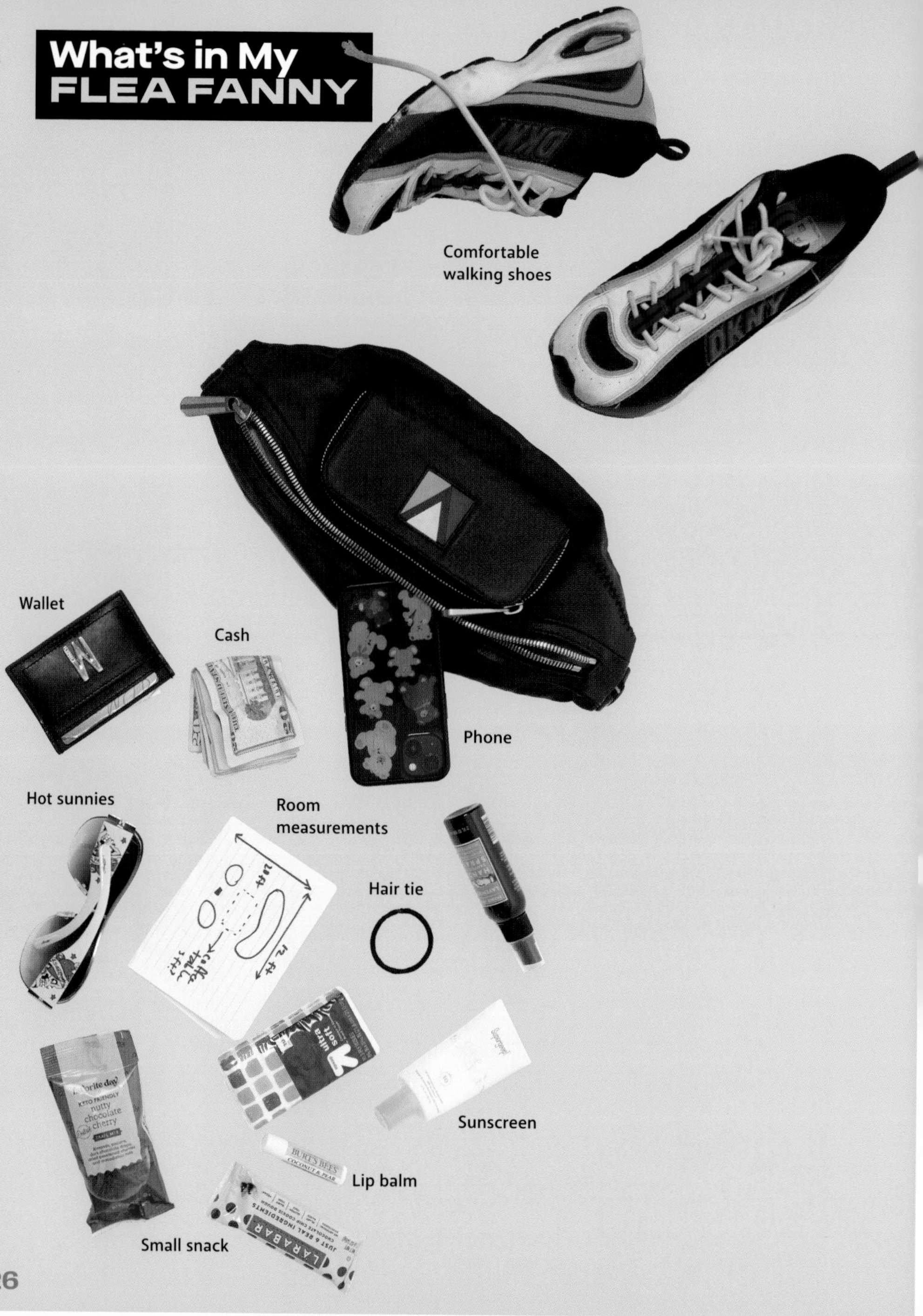

Comfortable walking shoes

Wallet

Cash

Phone

Hot sunnies

Room measurements

Hair tie

Sunscreen

Lip balm

Small snack

THE FUTURE OF THE FLEA/
HONORABLE MENTION

- Hot Girl Market (Los Angeles, CA; @hotgirlmarket)

- Thick Thrift LA (Los Angeles, CA; @thickthriftla)

- Lucky Stars Market (San Diego, CA; @luckystarsmarket)

Now that you've mastered almost every part of the secondhand-shopping world, it's time to talk about the glorious time capsules that are estate sales. Trust me: even if you're a beginner, you'll be navigating these homes and (much like me) obsessed with this unique way of shopping in no time!

CHA

8

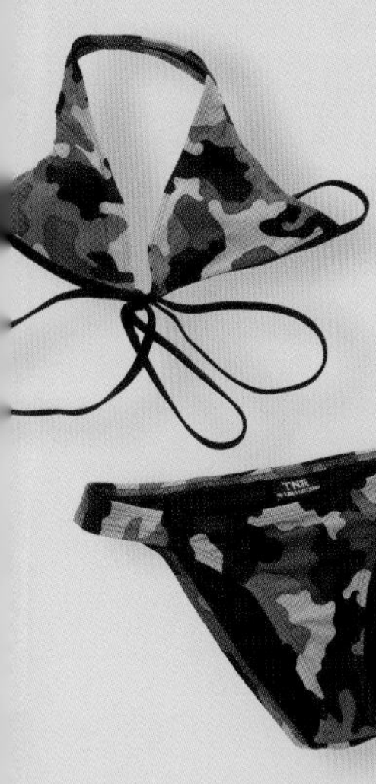

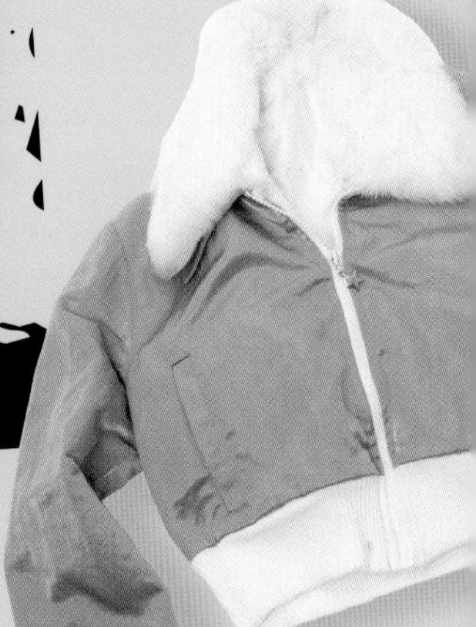

STER

Estate
SALES

WHILE THE TRIED-AND-TRUE THRIFT WILL FOREVER HOLD MY HEART, I BEGAN A GRAND LOVE affair with estate sales in 2020 and have been on quite a wild ride ever since. Over the past few years, I've spent countless hours rummaging through the homes of past adult-film stars, pageant queens, government officials, and even icons like the late Alex Trebek of *Jeopardy!* fame. In what other universe am I able to walk into the coveted home of a TV legend and casually leave with a vintage tracksuit from his personal wardrobe? (My best friend even snagged Trebek's director's-style chair, now living its new life in her downtown Los Angeles studio!)

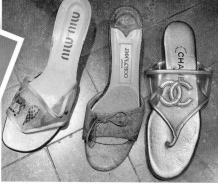

I've sifted through what feels like every antique drawer in and around LA, emerging with all the whos, whats, whens, wheres, and whys of the estate sale world. And I'm here to fill you in on the HOWS. But if you don't live in a big city, fear not! Estate sales are in towns all across the country. In fact, some of the best treasures are often found outside major cities. Don't discount the shoppable time capsule that is your neighbor's best friend's grandma's house! Buckle up, because this chapter is going to cover every question you've ever had on estate sales and how to shop them like a pro.

What IS an Estate Sale?

While we broke down the more *textbook* definition in chapter 1, let's dive deeper into what you can actually expect from this very unique type of shopping experience.

Estate sales, for the most part, are held when a person has passed, leaving a residence full of items behind. Homes, especially ones that have been well lived in for decades, accumulate a lot of stuff and the process of going through a recently deceased family member's belongings can of course be extremely personal, complicated, and overwheming. This is usually when an estate sale company is called in to curate the items and make them most salable, while simultaneously taking the burden off those moving or potentially grieving the loss of a loved one.

Now, there are definitely those who have the wrong impression of estate sales and what their true purpose is. I've gotten plenty of comments online saying how "morbid" or "wrong" it feels to walk through the house of a stranger and purchase their once-loved belongings. And yeah, I can see how the whole thing could sound weird to some, but Amy Byer, the owner of Handled, one of LA's most popular estate sale companies, has a unique perspective on this. Before Handled ever existed, Amy was a frequent estate sale shopper, never giving much thought to the support an estate sale could truly provide for a family facing hard times, that is, until her own loss led to a career change she never saw coming.

"My mother passed away and I suddenly had two houses to deal with. I had attended a lot of estate sales throughout my life but had never thought about it from a client's perspective," Byer said. She was so blown away by the service, the transparency, and how it allowed her to grieve the loss of her mother, knowing the estate sale company would take care of everything. This was the moment when Amy's life shifted in a new and totally unexpected direction. "I felt I had found my calling right then and there." Amy first began working for the company that had helped her through her mother's estate sale, but when that company shut down, Amy continued to get calls from others wanting her estate sale services. "From those previously formed relationships, I started my own business, Handled, here in LA, helping people with estate sales and I can't believe it. It's my life's calling and I love it, it has been incredible." Amy is now able to do what she loves, curating spaces with iconic wardrobes and timeless pieces, providing for others the same service that helped her so much in her own time of need. "I feel most excited when my clients have the same experience I had after my mom's passing—when people thank me and tell me that this has made it easier for them. It's everything to me. I just really love what I do."

Many who work in the estate sale industry refer to the *"Big D's"*—death, divorce, debt, and downsizing, the circumstances that can lead to the need for an estate sale. But before we go any further, let me spill on one of the best estate sales I have ever been to in my life.

I attended a sale in 2022 at the home of Allen Schwartz. Schwartz and his wife had moved out of their Mandeville Canyon ranch, leaving behind the most insane collection of everything you could possibly imagine, ready to be shopped at their four-day estate sale. Allen Schwartz is the designer behind the popular nineties brand ABS, a tag you've probably seen pop up at a thrift store from time to time. I had scored a ton of their pieces in the past. But nothing prepared me for what I would find at this estate sale.

Where Do You FIND THEM?

Here are the main ways to find estate sales in your area.

ESTATESALES.NET

It may look like one of the first websites ever made, but I adore the simplicity of it. It's a bit daunting to navigate at first, but once you get into a rhythm, this will be your destination for all things estate sales and your best friend when maneuvering this sometimes chaotic pastime. (There is also estatesales.org, which delivers a similar setup and listings, but overall I find estatesales.net easier to sift through.)

Now let's do this together! Pull up estatesales.net and key in your zip code or **(HOT TIP)** the name of the most "fancy" or well-off neighborhood in your area.

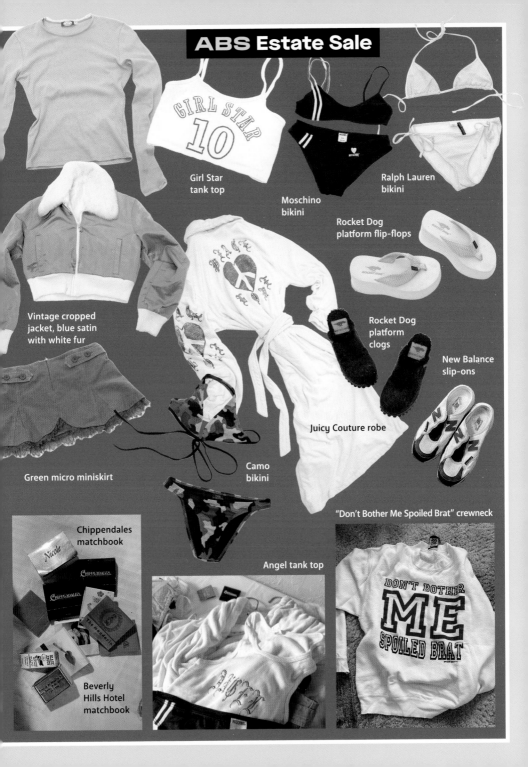

ABS Estate Sale

Girl Star tank top

Moschino bikini

Ralph Lauren bikini

Rocket Dog platform flip-flops

Rocket Dog platform clogs

New Balance slip-ons

Vintage cropped jacket, blue satin with white fur

Juicy Couture robe

Green micro miniskirt

Camo bikini

"Don't Bother Me Spoiled Brat" crewneck

Chippendales matchbook

Angel tank top

Beverly Hills Hotel matchbook

When you're on the page for the area you want to search, look to the left side, where you're going to first click "Date Then Distance." I tend to keep this toggle checked, so I get a good combination of sales happening ASAP and listings no farther than an hour or so away.

Next you'll need to decide which types of sales you want to sift through. Contrary to what the name might suggest, the site isn't just for estate sale listings. If you look over to the left side of the page you'll see a slew of categories that read: "Estate Sales," "Auctions," and "Additional Liquidations." Those three categories are then broken up into subcategories, offering you the option to check or uncheck the types of sales you'd like to shop:

ESTATE SALES

Estate Sales	Warehouse
Moving Sales	By Appointment
Moved Off Site to	Online Estate Sales

AUCTIONS

Auctions	Online Only Auctions
Auction House	

ADDITIONAL LIQUIDATIONS

Business Closings	Single Item Type Collections
Moved Off Site to Store	Buyouts or Cleanouts
Outside Sales	Demolition Sales

This is all personal preference, which you'll develop as you become more acquainted with this way of shopping, but if your mission is to start with a classic estate sale experience, uncheck all but "Estate Sales" and "Moving Sales" for the best results.

Once you have all your listings in front of you, it's time to explore. Roll and scroll. When you land on a sale that excites or intrigues you, dig even further. Most of your questions about the sale will be answered throughout the listing. The "Terms & Conditions" section will usually give you the specifics on forms of payment they prefer or are accepting, whether there will be an early-bird sign-up sheet or not, when that sign-up sheet will go out, if you can bring in a purse or not, etc. Following that, the "Description & Details" drop-down will give you a description of the items available and may mention who the previous owners were if it's of special note or relevance to the sale.

> # -HOT TIP-
>
> ## DESCRIPTION & DETAILS... ALWAYS TAKE A CLOSER LOOK!
>
> This is the section to pay attention to if you are going for something specific. For example, if you're only interested in clothing, look for descriptions like "vintage clothing galore" or "packed wardrobe." Next, you'll look through any photos the company posted of the sale. The photos don't always reflect every piece that sale has to offer, but out of the photos posted, often everything shown, including that gorgeous lamp in the background of the main living room shot, will be for sale. So, make sure to do a little squinting and you may find a hidden gem no one else in line even saw!

EMAIL LISTS

Get on those email lists! Though a few sites may hold the actual listing for the estate sale, getting on a specific company's email list can come with its own set of perks. "My company sends out the address of our sales early to those customers subscribed to our email list," Byer shared with me in discussing her tips for potential estate sale shoppers. This gives those who subscribed a chance to get over to the sale early and get their name at the top of the sign-up sheet. And trust me, that is a place you definitely want to be.

An efficient way to find out what companies have email lists and how to get on them is to first compile a few of the listings you've found on estatesales.net in your area. Follow this up by creating a list of the estate sale companies listed as hosting the specific sales you saved. Then search for those companies' websites and Instagram pages (most tend to have some kind of presence on social media these days). This is where you'll be able to scope out any information available on how to get on their particular mailing lists.

WHEN Are We Shopping?

So you've found a few sales you're interested in hitting, but what's the sweet spot when it comes to arrival? This will of course vary, but most estate sales span a weekend, giving you anywhere from two to four days to shop. I'm going to give you my personal rule of thumb when it comes to figuring out when to set out on your estate sale mission.

Say you came across a listing and scoped out an iconic treasure you absolutely must have. It's a specific midcentury-modern coffee table you never expected to come across, an eighties floor lamp so perfect you may pass out right then and there, maybe even a vintage Chanel bag you have been eagerly trying to thrift manifest for years. Go early! The notable pieces, especially those pictured in the listing, will go fast, and the more you go, the more you'll start to recognize the same few early birds around the front of the line each time. These are mostly going to be your area's collectors, resellers, dealers, and other vintage fanatics like myself. These people are usually looking for the higher-ticket items and probably care less about random closet finds and trinkets. However, getting chummy with these folks can definitely pay off. More on that below.

At my core, I am an early bird. If there is a hot find to be had, I will raise my booty well before the sun is up and speed over to get my name on that list or spot near the front of the line. Not to be too dramatic, but this isn't for the faint of heart, and those with tiny bladders, beware! (Remember, there is the drive to the sale *and* a line to get in once you arrive. Most homes will not have a bathroom available for use, so it may be a few hours till you next see one.)

Another thing about early birds: some people may use items like boxes, water bottles, any miscellaneous thing from their car to hold their place in line if they're there before a sign-up sheet even comes out. Think of this practice as a "pre-line" shoppers will sometimes form to create an order to sign up in once the official sign-up sheet from the estate sale company is eventually put out.

On the flip side, say the sale looks good but there isn't a specific item you're after. You feel like digging for a deal but want less of the line-related muss and fuss. Your sweet spots are going to be:

1. An hour before closing on the first day of the sale. Some of the most sought-after items will probably be long gone in the early hours but there will still be plenty of finds to be uncovered, minus the big-ass crowd.

2. For the most part, estate sale companies roll out discounts as the days pass. For example, the first day will always be full price, second could be 25 percent off, third maybe 50 percent off, and the last day sometimes as high as 75 percent off everything! "If you're really looking for the best deal, come on the last day when prices are less firm and things will be more negotiable," says Amy. More specifically, if you are hoping to tap some estate sales to furnish your new pad, the larger, harder-to-move items like couches, armoires, dressers, and beds are the pieces usually left on the last day of the sale, with the smaller items usually going first, as not everyone has the transportation needed to move the larger items on-site. Amy agrees: "Coming in the very last hour on the last day of sale, you can find some incredible deals on large items to furnish your space."

3. There really is no bad time to go to an estate sale. And if you can't make it in the time slots suggested above or happen to drive by a sign screaming your name from the side of the road, go! What's meant for you will find you and at the end of the day, the secondhand universe works in mysterious ways. You never know what's out there waiting for you to come swoop it up and make it your own.

Time to SHOP!

You've got a few sales in mind and have chosen your day to venture out. Now what?

- **Hit the ATM before you hit the sale.** These days many do accept digital payment or cards but in the estate sale world cash is king and will almost always be the preferred method of payment. (**HOT TIP:** There will be some estate sale listings that are extremely vague. They may have little to no description, and while that is not a reason to write them off, it is safe to assume a sale with little to no description may be cash-only, so come prepared.)

- **Be kind in line.** Not to beat a dead pair of Manolos, but I'm telling you, secondhand shopping karma is very real. Like I said above, you'll start seeing the same people as you begin to frequent sales in your area and it definitely doesn't hurt to become friendly with those familiar faces. LA-based vintage collector and frequent estate sale shopper Quinn Garvey uttered a similar sentiment to me: "Get on everyone's good side, especially those sometimes older early birds. There will come a time when they will help you out because they aren't looking for the same things as you. They are looking for some ceramic vase, not a vintage Juicy tracksuit or a trendy table." I have to agree. I had an experience like this a while back with a really kind man, around my grandparents' age, whom I had become chummy with from previous sales. He ran up to find me in the wardrobe room at a sale just to give me a bedazzled Dior tank top he found in the basement while looking through the art. Another note on lines: depending on the ways of the company holding the sale or size of the home, there can be circumstances where they only let a certain number of people in at a time (sometimes for a certain amount of time but I will say this is rare in my experience), which is why it's good to know what you're potentially after, helping to maximize your time in the home!

- **Have a plan of attack.** Similar to the thrift store, have a little list on hand to help keep track of what you are searching for. This list should include all that you are currently trying to thrift manifest but also those mundane household items like brooms, bowls, silverware, Swiffers. All of those random items we need but are annoying to spend money on.

- **Check every single (not-taped-off) drawer, closet, cabinet, and hidden compartment.** One of my best estate sale scores to date is a pair of dainty vintage Dior sleep shorts I found balled up in one of the dressers in the bathroom of the home. They had created a separate area of the house (as some will) for the higher-end or designer items, but someone must have missed the shorts when setting up and they ended up letting me scurry off with them for only two dollars! I smiled all day long.

- **Locate the hold table.** As the finds pile up in your arms, it will get increasingly difficult to keep digging. Most sales will have a hold table in a certain room or by the checkout. These are spots where you can leave items you're looking to purchase, adding to your hold pile as you shop. For the most part, shoppers respect the hold table and will abide by the estate sale honor code, but if there is an item of high value (monetarily or in your heart) keep it in your hands just in case! (Most estate sales will also allow or sometimes even encourage you to bring boxes to carry your finds.)

- **Be friendly with the staff.** I always think it's common sense to be kind to those who have spent days, sometimes weeks taking a packed house and transforming it into an experience for you to enjoy. But alas, the entitlement and overall-not-so-nice energy I've seen slung at those working estate sales from potential customers are quite icky. I like to think of it as an immense privilege to be given the opportunity to sift through someone's once-cherished belongings and give them new life.

- **Barter respectfully.** Pricing is another important aspect of estate sales (obviously we all want a good deal!) that will always differ, depending on a few different factors. I've been to a plethora of sales that mirror more "yard-sale-type pricing." Many have clothing items from $1 to $5, with larger pieces like furniture and décor for under $100. But there will be some sales, especially those with archive designer clothing, rare art pieces, high-end furniture, etc., that can definitely lean toward the more pricey side. This isn't without reason. When it comes to the pricing strategy at Amy's company, she wants shoppers to know that "the families that hire us are trying to raise money. I, of course, want it to be a good experience for the buyers, those shopping the sale, but I have to first focus on the seller, who is in possession of these items. I want them to have the experience they need primarily. I balance all of those different aspects when selling the items and it's a tricky dance." However, kind and respectful bartering is most always welcome. If there is a specific item you are going in for, come with *comps* to show those running the sale and you may be able to come to a price that works out for everyone. Again, kindness

here is key. Think about it: someone is much more likely to give a discount or come down in price for a shopper who has genuine love for a piece and is treating the items, home, and estate sale staff with care and respect.

- **Be prepared.** If you're going for furniture, have a plan for how you'll transport it home and keep in mind the cost of a potential truck rental when deciding how much to spend on a piece. Additionally, have a tape measure on hand to make sure your find will fit in your space.

- **Assess the vibes.** If you dug how the sale went or the vibe of the home, checking out at the register is the time to ask about any email lists or social pages they may have.

WHAT to Buy?

For some it's the clothes (hi, hello, me!), while for others it's eccentric art, vintage furniture, or even just your most basic everyday appliances. I actually got my current vacuum cleaner at an estate sale in Calabasas, California, two years ago for ten dollars and it's still zooming along strong. I know we've talked endlessly in this book about clothing because, I mean, I fucking love clothes. And while estate sales have opened the doors to some of the most miraculous closets I have ever laid eyes on, never mind had at my fingertips, one thing the estate sale world truly introduced into my life was the ability to create a secondhand home, full from frame to frame with my dream furniture finds.

Since I was a teen, I've dabbled in the home sections of countless thrift stores, picking up little vases, dishes, glassware, with the occasional side table or chair. But up until 2020, I had never had a pad with enough room to create a space that truly felt like home. I moved into a one-bedroom, one-bathroom apartment in West Hollywood that I shared with my boyfriend, Tyler. It was our second place together after spending our first three years in LA in a five-hundred-square-foot studio apartment. Upon signing the lease, I dreamed of filling it with furniture scores from thrifts and fleas all across LA. I had such a specific vision for what I could bring to life in a home filled with pre-loved pieces. However, as move-in day approached, there was increasing chatter surrounding the coronavirus and how it was going to affect our daily lives. As we got into bed on night one in our new place, the mayor of LA announced that the city was officially under lockdown. As the months passed and our asses stayed put in our completely unfurnished home, I longed for the day that at the time I thought may never come, when the thrift stores would reopen and I could finally secure my secondhand finds. Of course, I had been tempted to buy items from IKEA and the ease that comes with ordering something to be delivered right to your doorstep. But the thrift queen inside me told me to wait it out in our pretty empty place and I'm damn grateful that I did.

Then came yet another day at home near the end of May 2020. I was scrolling through my Instagram feed for what felt like the fiftieth time that afternoon, staring longingly at vintage furniture I dreamed would one day fill

my apartment, when I came across a local vintage store that just happened to share a post about an estate sale they were going to the next day. At this point the thrift stores around me had not opened back up and the thought of leaving my four walls to be around humans *and* used things felt extremely exhilarating. I had been to a few estate sales back in Ohio but nothing could have prepared me for the world I was about to enter. I masked up, made my way over to the breathtaking LA neighborhood that is Brentwood, and got my booty in line. They required masks, took our temperatures at the door, and only allowed five people to enter the home at a time. I was more than thrilled to do whatever would get me out of my house and into this one. One hour later I surfaced with two Yves Saint Laurent tops, a Dior sweater vest, and countless home décor pieces, all for the grand total of thirty dollars.

In the year that followed, I hustled to roughly three estate sales every weekend, and piece by piece my vision for my pre-loved pad started to come to life. It felt like my Pinterest board (which I had been using to manifest my dream home finds, duh!) had come to life right in front of my face. And when I asked Quinn for her two cents on what you should always be checking estate sales for first, she felt similarly. "I always tell anyone and everyone looking to furnish their space that the furniture at estate sales will just blow your mind. Every Pinterest board you make, any inspo you have, *this* is the next step to seeing how someone actually styled that authentic 'made in Denmark' piece in their home."

If you need any more convincing, let me remind you that while secondhand shops are amazing and full of treasures, said treasures are donations—items that someone has either given away or consigned. They're pieces that someone has gotten rid of. Estate sales, however, are full of items that have been held on to and cherished, and have truly stood the test of time.

HOW TO Shop an Estate Sale Wardrobe

All estate sales are going to be set up differently based on the layout of the home, the items available, and the preference of the client and estate sale company putting it on. Generally, housewares, knickknacks, and furniture will be sprinkled about in various locations, but clothing is a whole other beast. Depending on the clothing/accessory contents of the sale, I've found that if there is a massive collection of garments or extremely high-end designer pieces, there is most likely going to be a designated "wardrobe room," containing all the fashion goods the home has to offer. And as mentioned above, the description on the listing will almost always give you prior insight on the details of the sale. I usually make a beeline right for that room, where from time to time (based on the physical size of the home or amount of people they are letting in to shop at a time) there will be a slight line to enter, but I find this to be pretty rare. Most times, once you have made it into the sale, you are free to roam about (unless a room is taped off or sporting a sign saying "do not enter") and pick up your finds as you go. These types of wardrobe-centric rooms tend to be a bit more organized with clothing racks and stylized for more ease when moving through the merchandise.

On the flip side of the hanger, you have your can-be chaotic "digger's paradise," where there is pretty much zero organization and the home looks as if the owner was just there yesterday (sounds a bit morbid, I know, but sometimes this simply means the owner got up and moved, leaving all as is for the estate sale company to sell). This usually suggests no designated closet room and turns the shopping experience into a thrift trip turned all the way up. You've got to get down, dig, and keep an eye on your fellow shoppers digging right alongside you or peering over your shoulders at what you may have scored!

FACEBOOK Marketplace

Facebook Marketplace can get overlooked but is an incredible resource for finding unique pieces in your area. I find this platform is utilized more so by sellers itching to move something out of their home rather than trying to make as much money as possible. This is perfect for those of you furnishing your first apartment or for finding wild deals on *clothing lots* or designer pieces. Here are a few tips for navigating Facebook Marketplace:

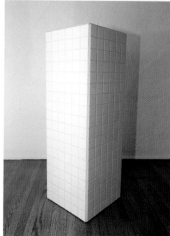

1. On Facebook you'll use the save feature to help the algorithm suggest similar pieces you may be interested in. I'm always searching up "Art Deco vintage furniture" for pieces to round out my space, and now Facebook is constantly serving me up pieces that match my personal vibe.

2. Broaden the radius of your search. Instead of ten miles try twenty, even thirty (truly whatever you're willing to drive), to allow for more items to pop up that may only be a few minutes outside that initial ten-mile marker.

3. Remember, it's not just home pieces; people list clothing and accessories as well. I don't do this super often but I will search up my more fashion-focused finds on Facebook Marketplace if my normal thrift spots aren't delivering a specific want.

4. Don't be shy about asking if they would be open to shipping the item. My sister and I recently had an extremely thrilling thrift manifestation moment, involving a pair of Y2K Ed Hardy boots for the cheapest price we had ever come across and a very kind lady. We had been searching for these furry tattooed babies for six months and when we finally came across them in our size *and* for only fifteen dollars we were not about to let the distance stand in our way. The boots were too far for us to drive to during the week, so we sent the seller a message exclaiming our love for the pair, offered to pay for the shipping, and she accepted! The worst they can say is no, so shoot your shot!

5. I'm not a fan of using the suggested message that pops up when you go to send, so create your own based on the details given by the seller. That way sellers do not mistake your message for spam.

6. Be as clear as possible. Ask whatever questions you have regarding the pieces, and express your genuine interest. Ask when the best time is for you to pick it up so they know you are serious and you stand out.

7. Once you send the message, be prepared to go swoop! There may be someone else in communication with that seller as well and sometimes it's truly a snooze-you-lose situation.

CHA

9

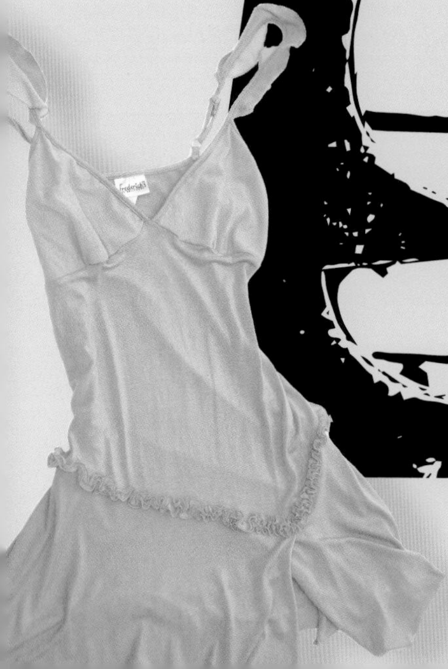

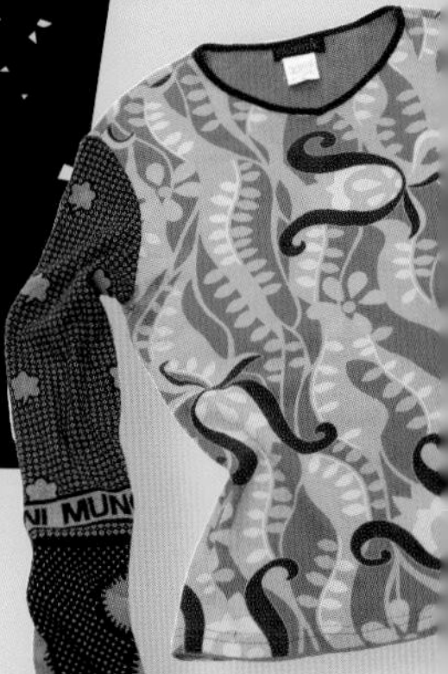

OTER

Any More QUESTIONS?

The new
Bisou-Bisou Girl
in town.

IN THIS NEVER-ENDING UNIVERSE OF CREATIVITY, CHAOS, AND FABULOUS FINDS, I COULDN'T POSSIBLY cover everything you should know or want to know without turning the mic over to you.

I asked for absolutely any and every question my followers have ever had about secondhand shopping and compiled them into the ultimate thrift Q&A.

How did you find your personal style?

Through thrifting it out! Like most of us, my personal style evolution has involved a lot of trial and error. Honestly, being open to "looking silly" or "out of place" and letting go of what others may think are key. It's fun to use trends and nostalgia for inspiration, but at the end of the day your personal style does not need to fit into a certain box or aesthetic. I started out on my style journey by thrifting tons of oversize eighties sweaters, vintage band tees, and high-waisted denim, solely because I was obsessed with eighties pop culture. Now, though, my style makes a ton of nods to the 1990s and early 2000s but is more rooted in what truly feels like me, not just trends or pieces I simply enjoy looking at.

Thrifting takes a lot of time and for those who don't have it, what's the best way to go about it?

Make a plan. I know a lot of you are busy working, taking care of your families, turning in assignments, etc. So pick a day when you do have a bit of time to spare, grab your thrift list, and focus on the sections that reflect the items you're actively chasing on that day.

I also recommend making thrifting less of a chore and more of an experience to share with your loved ones. Turning it into a fun thing to do with your kids, friends, or family members is a great way to maximize the little free time you may have. When my mom was busy working 24/7 and my sister and I were working while in school, our weekly trips to the thrift were sometimes the only quality time we got to have with each other, and it was always the best day of the week!

Macy's PERSONAL Style Journey

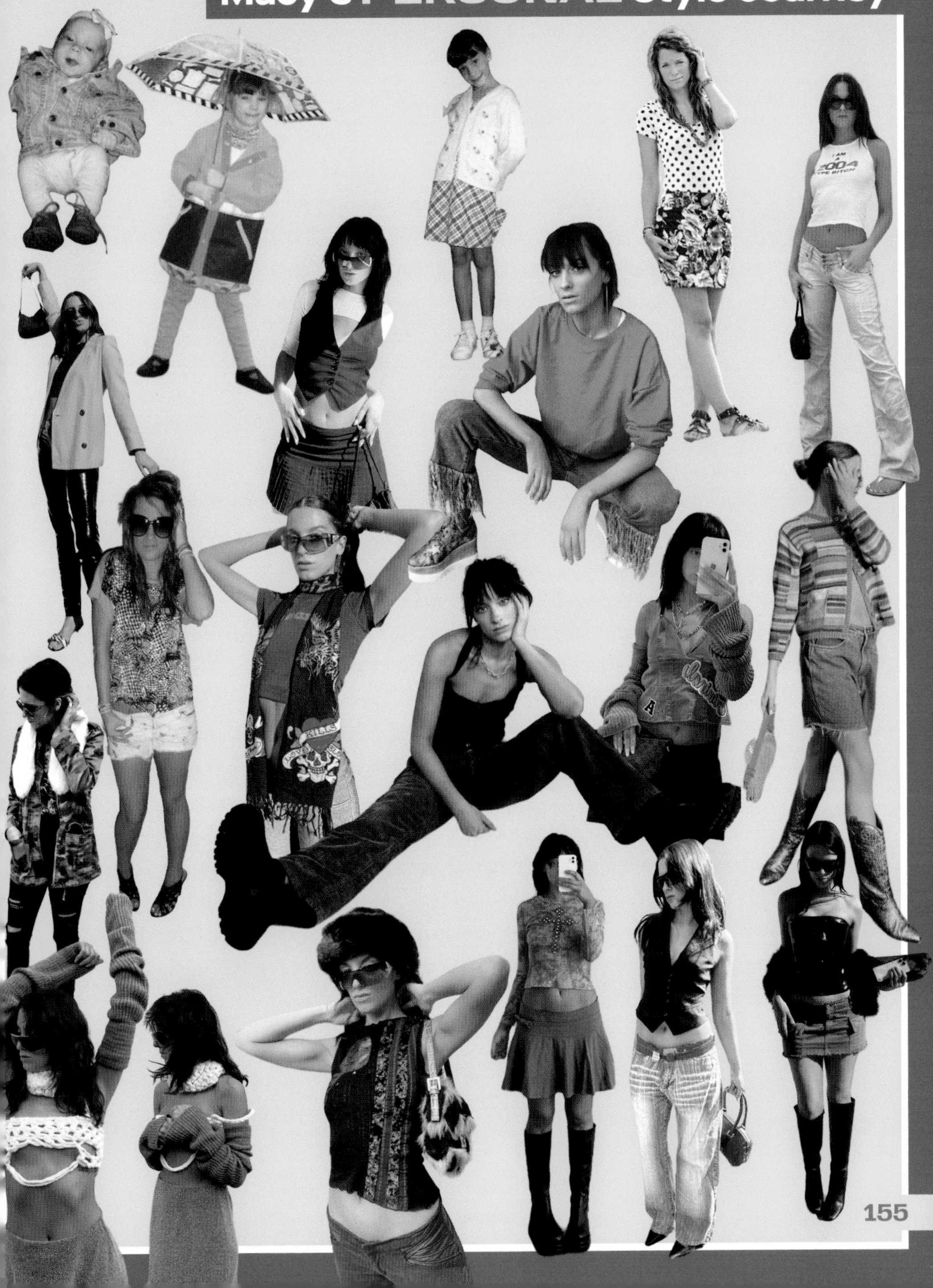

How do I decide whether or not to get a piece of clothing if I'm not sure?

Try to leave it behind. You have to be really honest with yourself here. If you can even remotely see it as a piece that may sit in a pile collecting dust in your closet, leave it for another thrift queen to find. Plus, this leaves you with more money in your thrift bag to get something you really love the next time around. The thrift gods are always looking out and will reward you for not buying every find in sight!

However, I will admit here and now that cute shoes are my weakness and I've often picked up a pair I knew were not my size, lying to myself that I could squeeze my foot in. It's not worth it, queen. Put it back.

What are ways to create good relationships with your regular thrift spots?

This is such a good question, and let me tell you, it absolutely pays to be on the employee's good side. A simple "Hi, how are you?" to the cashier as you enter the store is a great place to start. Taking that extra few seconds to show kindness to the person at the register or filling up the racks with glorious finds goes a long way. Beyond kind words, it's really all about being courteous and thoughtful in the thrift store atmosphere and community. It's the most basic of things, like picking up the fitting room after use and putting unwanted merchandise either back in the section you found it or on the rack of "go backs." Refrain from giving an innocent employee a hard time about the price of an item you think should be cheaper when they have absolutely no say in the matter themselves. The old guiding principle of treating others the way you'd like to be treated applies here. Oh, and please remove hangers from the pieces in your cart as you approach the line. This might feel small or obvious, but it's a strict thrift rule of mine. Several stores will have signs near the front requesting that you do remove them, but I can attest that it is truly appreciated at all spots and will keep the line moving much faster for everyone. As I said earlier, thrift karma is very real, and if you put out that positive energy, it will make its way back into your cart. Trust me!

Do you ever get overwhelmed when sifting through every single piece? How can you get through it?

I don't anymore but that is solely due to my experience and comfort level in thrift stores.

It's quite normal to feel a bit taken aback at the sight of racks upon racks, filled with sometimes thousands of random items for you to sift through. If you do feel overwhelmed, take a deep breath and try tackling one section at a time. Most thrift stores are organized by "type of item," with some breaking it down even further to divide by size or color. Pick three or four sections you want to shop that day and tune out the rest. I know this may feel like it contradicts the previous rule I gave in chapter 2, to "check every section," but in this case it's better to dial in on just a few racks to avoid getting frazzled and peacing out empty-handed.

How does location impact your thrift finds?

I'm a firm believer that it's not about where you go but how often you are out there thrifting and I think most experienced thrifters would agree. That said, you're definitely more likely to find designer pieces in more wealthy neighborhoods, vintage from the 1960, '70s and '80s, in towns with a high retirement population, and newer, day-to-day pieces (less picked over too!) in your more typical American suburbs. But don't get too caught up on location. There isn't a place in this world I wouldn't try thrifting in, because you truly never know until you look.

The thrifting is fabulous in LA, but there isn't a day I don't miss my hometown Ohio spots. Small-town thrifting rocks all the way in my book!

What are your favorite brands and fabrics?

BRANDS: Rampage, Bisou Bisou, LEI, Ed Hardy, Diesel, Wilsons Leather, Bebe, St. John's Bay, Morgan de Toi, 7 for All Mankind, Hot Kiss, Custo Barcelona, Anxiety Cafe, Harley-Davidson, Self Esteem, Guess, Miss Sixty, Juicy Couture, Cato, CLIO, Adidas, Lucky Brand, Hard Tail, RealTree, Newport News, Charles David (heels specifically), Baby Phat, vintage Forever 21, Betsey Johnson, Express, Versace Sport, DSquared2, Xhilaration . . . the list could go on, but these babies are always on my mind!

FABRICS: leather, denim, silk, cashmere.

Fredericks of Hollywood

Ed Hardy

Morgan de Toi

Hard Tail

Wilsons Leather

Bisou Bisou

The new Bisou-Bisou Girl in town.

Custo Barcelona

Harley-Davidson

HARLEY. DAVIDSON.

Miss Sixty

LOVE

Versace

VERSACE

Rampage

Von Dutch

Baby Phat

baby phat 21

TRASH

1969

Juicy Couture

Tripp NYC

ANY MORE QUESTIONS?

159

s BARN

KUSTOMMADE
Von Dutch.
ORIGINALS

A·B·S©
by Allen Schwartz

PS

The
Disney
Store

CONTEMPO
C A S U A L S

AUTHENTIC AMERICAN BRAND
PARIS BLUES
ORIGINALS
Fun fashion experience

Christian Dior
MONSIEUR

FASHION BUG ®

RSACE
COUTURE

Jag

BILLBLASS

Love P&G
JUICY COUTURE
MADE IN THE GLAMOROUS U.S.A.
S

MOSCHINO
JEANS

Hello Kitty

SEXY WOMAN

ie Lee
FOR
SOUTH

HOTKISS
U.S.A.

ries™

Lizsport

X·O·X·O

JUMP
Apparel Co.
by Wendye Chaitin
MADE IN U.S.A.

dd
ANS

Lovable.®

Sophia
by delicates©

Playmate

Salyers'
US·FURS

weeds
75% POLYESTER 85% COTTON

Bob Mackie
WEARABLE ART

TENDERLOIN
CALIFORNIA

How do you stay motivated to thrift when the thrifts around you aren't hitting?

Dry spells at the thrift store happen to us all (yes, even me!) and they are definitely a bummer. I know I'm always searching for that wow moment and when I'm met with pieces that aren't quite my jam, it's easy to get discouraged. I get it. But I think these dry spells come from sticking to the same spots too much and I always take it as a sign to search out a new one. I swear, even if you are the absolute thrift queen of your town and are like, "Macy, girl, I have been to every thrift store around me five times over," think again. There are always, and I mean *always*, new spots popping up, and ones that are so hidden, only a few are in the know. My sister reminded me that our favorite thrift store, American Thrift in Dayton, Ohio, became our go-to spot because of a dry spell! We had been thrifting in our hometown for years and years, when one day we were at our regular Salvation Army, not thrilled over what we were finding, and decided to ask another customer in the store where else they get their thrift on. The woman excitedly told us about a little spot that wasn't even listed on Google yet, swearing up and down it was The One. She did not oversell. It was incredible! And it has been our go-to thrift store ever since.

How can you tell a clothing item is vintage without knowledge of the brand?

Your phone is one of your biggest assets at the thrift store. I recommend looking up any brand you are unsure on, curious about, or obsessed with on Google, using descriptors relevant to the exact piece you found. You can sometimes find that same item or one similar listed somewhere with more information on the piece.

The Vintage Fashion Guild (vintagefashionguild.org) is an incredible free resource and has its own "Guide to Vintage Labels." There people can submit different vintage tags from countless brands with any information they may have on what decade it was created and/or sold. It's like a digital scrapbook of physical vintage tags, and if you're a frequent thrifter, you know how much we love to simply stare at and take in a good-ass tag.

How do you know if the find is ugly or fashionable?

The truth is, only you will know. We've all seen those pieces so ugly that we're like, "But is this so ugly it's cute?" If a unique piece catches your eye and you're unsure if you love it or hate it, pause for a moment and picture at least one outfit that you could put together using that item paired with pieces from your current wardrobe. Then, even if that piece is "so ugly" to some people, it doesn't matter one bit because you made it a *fit* and look absolutely fabulous!

When is the best time to thrift?

As soon as the thrift store opens. It's quiet, typically pretty empty, and a hell of a lot easier to navigate. I find that the first hour is the ultimate sweet spot, as more people tend to trickle in toward the late morning and early afternoon.

But if mornings aren't your jam, I'd recommend going around dinnertime. Most people are getting off work and going home to hang with their families or just relax, not hitting the thrift store. In the later hours there is typically different merchandise that wasn't out in the morning, along with the perk that some people have spent all day scouring the store, leaving tons of "go back" piles around on the racks. I truly love the magic that radiates off another thrift queen's "no pile." It can be a gold mine.

How do you prioritize pieces that align with your personal style as opposed to impulse-buying stuff because it's fun and cheap?

This is so important in the world of secondhand shopping and is something you will gain a deeper understanding of over time. When you're still in your newbie thrift era, it's inevitable you will purchase things you thought were bops that end up being items you just can't work into your wardrobe. And that's okay! Please don't be too hard on yourself. This is a learning experience, and as a wise East High Wildcat once said, we're all in this together! Remember, in an instance like this you can always re-donate, sell, or gift the piece to a friend. That's what is so beautiful about the circularity of the thrift store.

I'd also recommend taking a picture of the piece in question while you're at the thrift store. Who knows, maybe you'll find something that you dig by the same brand that rings truer to your personal style in a future thrift trip, or something with a similar vibe.

Do you set a budget for thrifting or just go for it?

I almost always set a budget! It is the key to staying focused on the pieces you truly want to add to your wardrobe versus just buying to buy. A budget helps me to be more intentional when hitting the racks and pushes me to snap inspo photos of the pieces I love that are out of my price range on that given day. If you run into a find you love that's priced too high, snap that pic, pull it up at home, and tap into the virtual thrift world we mastered together in chapter 7. That photo will be your guide to finding what is truly meant for you.

How do you cultivate your list of favorite thrift spots? Trial and error? Reviews? Word of mouth?

All of the above! Everyone is going to have a different opinion based on their personal style, what they're searching for, how they like to shop, etc. I have my go-to faves, of course, but when I'm looking to branch out and find new spots to shop, I pick a town anywhere up to thirty miles outside of my current city and simply plug "thrift stores" into Google Maps. From there I'll scroll the reviews, always looking for the spots the locals say are their favorites.

THE TOP 10 THINGS
I HAVE EVER THRIFTED

1. My Wilsons Leather moto jackets

2. Two Helmut Lang slip dresses, one black and one white, that I found at an Out of the Closet in West Hollywood

3. Fabulous blue Cavalli pants, from Valley Value Center in North Hollywood

4. Vintage Skechers sneaker heels from eBay, duh

5. Dior sunglasses

6. A vintage fur coat gifted to Pamela Des Barres (the world's most famous groupie, whose wardrobe I have had the absolute pleasure of visiting to shop) by one of the many rock legends she spent time with in the 1970s

7. All of my vintage Queen band tees

8. My black-label vintage Forever 21 pieces

9. Silver Gucci bag

10. My iconic giant high-heel shoe chair

ANY MORE QUESTIONS?

How do smaller thrift shops compare and compete with bigger corporate thrift stores like Goodwill and Savers?

If given the option, I am always going to choose a local mom-and-pop thrift store over any corporate spot. Most times, the prices will be cheaper because an independently owned store has a lower overhead cost than that of a Goodwill or Savers. Corporate thrift stores tend to be more tidy and organized but you are paying a higher price tag for an easier shopping experience. For beginners or those a little wary of the thrift world, ease in with a more corporate spot and gradually make your way to a local dig.

Do you wash everything when you buy it?

Have I worn a top straight out of my Goodwill bag because I had somewhere to be and no time left to launder? Yep. But do I clean every single one of my secondhand finds? Of course. But let's just go ahead and bust the myth right now that clothes from the thrift store are really that much dirtier than clothes that are, say, manufactured in factories, where workers are being mistreated, in conditions many would deem unlivable. I personally get a little bothered by the stigma around the supposed lesser "cleanliness" of secondhand shopping in general and it's one I really do hope to shift. I've been hearing "but clothes from the thrift store are so gross" ever since high school and it's a narrative extremely entrenched in classism. Our capitalist society has influenced the masses into believing we need everything "fresh" and "clean," leaving people to then associate the opposite of those words with used items and the people who buy them.

"That time I found Pucci jellies at an estate sale!"

How do you feel when you find a dream item?

If I'm alone, I quite literally sweat, shake, and pace around the store, internally screaming at the top of my lungs "Thank you!" to the thrift gods. But if I'm with my mom, my sister, or a friend, I usually rip it off the rack really fast, gasp for air, and bolt over to wherever they are to revel in the moment.

Which day of the week is best for thrifting?

You've got a few options:

1. The day your favorite thrift store puts out their new merchandise. Note, some spots are constantly putting out new pieces all day, every day, but I'd ask an employee next time you're there when they restock.

2. The best discount days! Again, don't be afraid to chat with the employees and inquire about what day they recommend coming in for the best deals.

3. There is no "bad day" to thrift. Do what works for you and your schedule and go when you have the day off work or can get away for a few hours.

Is thrifting a fake designer bag "bad," and how do you spot one at a thrift store?

The practice of creating and distributing counterfeit luxury bags is illegal and also deeply rooted in the same unethical practices as the fast-fashion clothing industry. That being said, they do exist and thrift stores are absolutely riddled with them. Similar to how I feel with regard to picking up ultra fast-fashion clothing items from the secondhand market, I'd much rather see these fake bags being used and passed to the next person as opposed to filling up a landfill. The reality is, people are buying these fakes from a multitude of sketchy sites online, so if you've been considering making that kind of purchase, look to the thrift store instead. Given how spot-on counterfeit bags have become in recent years, it has only gotten more difficult to tell them apart from the real thing. I've purchased my fair share of faux designer bags from secondhand shops over the years. If you're struggling to tell and the price is right, it's sometimes worth snagging and taking home to research further or be authenticated.

What are you always on the lookout for?

Leather jackets. I'm addicted and will search through them no matter the season.

How do you get so lucky?

I was kissed by the thrift gods at birth. Just kidding (kind of), but I've also spent a good portion of my life in thrift stores, honing the skills needed to find what I love the most. Thrifting is one of those things you truly do get better at as you put in more time and effort. And if you treat secondhand shopping like you would any hobby or skill you are trying to master, you will find yourself getting "luckier" too. Think of it like trying to get better at pottery or learning another language. Set aside one day a week, pick three thrift spots you want to explore, and dive in! We all have to start somewhere, and hell, you already have this book, so not one of you is starting from zero.

What's your white whale? The thing you've always hoped to find, even though it's like one in a million?

Anything—and I mean anything—from Tom Ford's 1990s–early 2000s Gucci era (specifically the infamous G-logo G-string from the spring–summer 1997 show). Ford was the brand's creative director from 1994 to 2004, bringing endless inspiration and some of the most sickening pieces I have ever seen walk a runway in my life. Think endless cutouts, plunging necklines, bold velvet, and sheer staples. Sharp, sophisticated, and mega sexy. You can definitely locate some of the pieces in the virtual thrift word, but I'm waiting it out for the day I find something on the racks!

How do you know if something will fit without being able to try it on?

Make sure you have your measuring tape on hand and are aware of your own measurements. This is when wearing a good thrift outfit comes into play (flip back to chapter 2 for more on this). In this case, you can also try utilizing the *neck test*, which is a general rule of thumb (but not foolproof!) that if you wrap the waistband on a pair of bottoms around your neck and the two ends perfectly meet, then they should fit around your waist.

What is the best thrift store you have ever been to?

American Thrift in Dayton, Ohio, hands down.

How much does the newfound popularity of thrifting affect its accessibility?

The popularity of thrifting has certainly risen but thrifting is still nowhere near the "norm." Contrary to what some may think, there are actually not enough people open to buying items secondhand. I won't ever discourage someone from buying used. It's the most inclusive and accessible way for one to shop more ethically and sustainably. However, it is important to be aware of the communities you are entering as a guest to shop in. Give back, bring donations, shop thoughtfully, and encourage more people to thrift!

Any thoughts on inheriting the energy of the previous owner of your thrift finds or them being haunted?

I'm really not a big fan of the idea of not shopping secondhand because of "bad vibes" items may or may not give off. I find it to be a pretty silly excuse to not use the billions of things that already exist on this planet. Remember that everything we put on our bodies, bring into our homes, and/or casually brush up against has, for the most part, been touched by someone else.

If this is what has held you back from thrifting, try to switch up your mindset. Think less "haunted" and more "enchanted." Remember, there's something magical about a piece being rescued from its probable end and being given new life by you!

How long does an average thrifting sesh take? How much time should one set aside to thrift?

This will depend on your experience level, but I can usually scan a full store within thirty minutes to an hour. But if you're more of a beginner, give yourself the afternoon to really get to know the shop you're in and where they keep things. You'll naturally start to get a rhythm going and get in and out much faster.

Do you care about overall wear and tear (fading, pilling, etc.) when thrifting?

It depends on the item and its purpose. If it's a pair of pajama pants I really dig but it has a hole or bit of pilling, I'll probably still get it. If it's a vintage band tee, I actually prefer it to be worn in and faded out. But when it comes to a piece that can't be saved using our methods from chapter 6, it should probably be left behind. Trust me, there have been plenty of times that I've found an item by an iconic designer or brand that I love but needed to be very real with myself that it was indeed tattered to bits. It should be left for someone who can really give it another life. Not every find is meant to be your next DIY project and that's okay.

Is there a point where thrifting becomes not sustainable anymore, such as buying too much, too often, and overconsuming?

I don't think I'd say "not sustainable anymore," but of course overconsumption can occur during any type of buying practice. I believe the key is striving to remain thoughtful and circular with your purchases, whether you are buying items to resell or for personal use. I can't lie: it's easy to go overboard at the thrift, but the point of this way of shopping is not to buy as many items as possible, but rather to thrift the items you need or that bring you joy! I'm no stranger to a big hot thrift haul but if you refer back to the closet cleanout we did earlier in this book, you'll have the tools to ensure your items continue living it up far past your purchase.

Secondhand
OUTFIT EQUATIONS

NOW THAT YOU'VE GOT ALL MY THRIFT TIPS AND TRICKS UNDER YOUR (EXTREMELY STYLISH secondhand) belt, we are going to put those future finds and closet staples to use with a few key secondhand outfit equations.

As I've said, I have always been deeply inspired by the pages of retro magazines. The layouts, silly playful descriptions, and sheer *fun* that was had with the clothing being presented to the consumer. Those pages played such a large role in influencing how I styled the thrift finds in my closet and I hope this section will feel reminiscent for you. My goal is to help eliminate a bit of stressing around dressing and provide a more visual look at working used clothing and accessories into your routine. Even as someone totally fashion obsessed, I can so relate to the ease all of us want to feel when getting dressed every day. It is such a crap feeling to be super excited for a date, work event, vacation, or girls' night out only to be brought down by the sheer chaos and stressful energy that come along with figuring out what to wear . . . especially if the look you were planning in your head doesn't turn out as expected.

When in a style pinch, the thrift store (or the countless resale sites we've touched on) has you covered and I'm here to send you off with a plethora of outfit equations that you can without a doubt score in the secondhand space, while at the same time utilizing items already in your wardrobe.

SECOND CHANCES

OFFICE **OUTFIT**

Bring on the businesswoman special—officewear, a wardrobe staple for many but typically not the most fun thing to purchase. We switch jobs, dress codes change, and we're expected to dress the part (even if our paycheck doesn't quite reflect room for new purchases). This is a category of dressing where the thrift store (physical and virtual) shines. Sleek and chic silhouettes from the 1980s, '90s, and early 2000s cover the racks at the thrift and will have you feeling like your most serious Romy & Michele selves in no time, while leaving you with a few more shekels in your pocket to spend on pieces you actually want to wear.

DATE NIGHT OUTFIT

I've been in a relationship for over a decade, so my date nights tend to lean more to the casual side of things. However, I do live with my younger sister, who is in her early twenties and heads out on spur-of-the-moment dates multiple times a week. Together we have concocted an accessible yet, of course, hot and fabulous outfit equation for your date night! I believe the biggest key to the date night look (or any look, for that matter) is feeling like yourself. It's not the time to pull out your most uncomfortable shoe or top that you have to keep adjusting throughout the night. I advise grabbing at least one item that you feel just so fucking confident in and building out the rest of the outfit around that piece.

Be it the perfect pair of jeans, a slinky black dress that fits like a damn glove, or a two-piece matching set for ease, the thrift has your back!

COLLEGE CLASS OUTFIT

College days are routinely spent moving from classroom to classroom in different buildings across campus, and the temperatures of those rooms are most definitely going to vary. I remember frequently freezing my ass off in a lecture I had walked to in the 85-degree heat, only to bop into a lab where the AC was broken. The goal is to have one outfit to carry you throughout your entire day, without having to stop back at your dorm room or apartment to change. Obviously we all have our slob-kabob days but admittedly, I always felt a little less sleepy and sluggish when I'd skip the sleepwear and opt for a look that provided a bit more energy. You definitely do not have to compromise comfort for style. Trade in your cotton joggers for a more sophisticated swoosh in your step.

HIGH SCHOOL
OUTFIT

In high school, I had two modes: rolling-out-of-bed chic (lol, I wish) and (attempting) to dress for success. High school is tricky. You're trying to figure out who you are, what you like, and what you feel comfortable in, as well as what you don't, all while trying to adhere to the rules of the dreaded dress code. Enter the maxi skirt. Now, I thought maxi skirts were a bit drab back in my high school days, but I'll admit that I was seriously misinformed. They come in such a plethora of different colors, styles, fabrics, prints, etc., and can provide optimal comfort while sitting in a chilly classroom or gabbing with your friends at the lockers. The secondhand long skirt can be dressed down, throwing on a fitted hoodie and sneakers, or up with a cute little cardigan and ballet flats.

HOT TIP: Look for one made out of similar material to your fave pair of sweatpants, with an elastic waistband. This will be your new sweat skirt and a new (to you) wardrobe staple.

GNO OUTFIT

Time to let your hair down, throw on your Bradshaw best, and have a night out with your friends! Think of this as your opportunity to pull out your most fun thrift finds—an animal print dress, sparkly sequin mini, or sky-high pink platforms. You don't waste those style scores on a date because they'd never appreciate the look quite as much as your hot hype squad will.

SECOND CHANCES

HOLIDAY PARTY OUTFIT

Each year, as Thanksgiving comes to a close and the holiday party invites come rolling in, there is an overwhelming amount of "holiday looks" being advertised by every brand out there. This push in marketing is to convince us that we need yet another shiny new dress or ugly holiday sweater. And guess what? We've all been subscribing to this "need new now" way of shopping for so many holiday seasons that your local thrift store or favorite resale site is bound to be packed full of last year's drops. This is the perfect opportunity for those of you whose interest in secondhand clothing has been piqued throughout this book to hit the thrift, estate sale, or local consignment shop and dig out those showstopping pieces for whatever events are on your calendar.

VACATION OUTFIT

Oh yes—the classic vacay slay. Going on a quick beach getaway or European summer trip is yet another occasion we've been collectively convinced we need a mini new wardrobe for, but nope, not this year! We're calling on the skirt section for the perfect white linen moment, tube tops, tanks, and versatile accessories like scarves that won't take up much space in your suitcase but can be transformed into tops (using the thrift flip you learned in chapter 7), and vintage/ deadstock swimsuits. I know that thrifted bathing suits may not be everyone's cup of tea—I can feel some of you curling your toes from here—but again, these gently used garments aren't any "dirtier" than, say, a bikini hanging up at Target that's been tried on by ten different people in its first day out on the floor. Much like a bathing suit at the thrift store, you don't know where the seemingly "new" one was or what it touched before making its way into your home and onto your bod. So, please do yourself a favor and do not sleep on the crazy amount of gently used or totally untouched deadstock vintage swim. Consider this your warning. You are about to look extremely fabulous.

DAY OFF OUTFIT

The recipe for a perfect day off outfit requires replacing the pieces you've been forced to wear all week with the items you may have less freedom to sport on the corporate court. It's most likely the weekend and you're off to the flea market or brunch with friends. Maybe you're going to the movies or simply bopping around your neighborhood catching up on your favorite pod goss. Wherever is on your list of errands, the day off *fit* is about you doing you. Pull out your grungy grandpa leather jacket, baggy vintage jeans (hell, sweatpants or comfy shorts if you just can't even with denim today), sneakers or boots, huge shield sunnies, whatever *you* want to wear . . . and toss it on!

The SPOTS 2 Shop

You didn't think I'd leave you hanging without a full and fabulous list of my must-hit secondhand spots to shop across the States, did you?

Sadly, I have yet to thrift in every corner of the country (keep an eye out for that one day on your TV screens!), but I do have a troop of extremely well-dressed, uniquely fashionable thrift queens surrounding me at all times (IRL as well as in the digital world) and collectively we are here to spill.

Whether you're hitting a big city for vacay, traveling to the most random state on the map for work, or exploring your own backyard, let's talk spots to shop. Get in, queens, we're going thrifting!

Locations and hours may change, so do a quick Google search before taking off.

LOS ANGELES

The one thing I miss about Ohio (besides, of course, my cutie-ass mom, Marilyn) is the thrifting. It fostered my creativity and was such a lifeline for my adolescent soul. Moving from Ohio to Los Angeles, a place I had never thrifted in a day in my life, felt equal parts exhilarating and totally daunting. I only knew of the places most tourists chattered about or that were featured in the movies, Melrose Avenue, of course. But I needed to pin down my go-to Goodwill, the best flea market to stroll on a Sunday, the spots that would surprise me time and time again, while also providing that familiar sense of comfort I crave when thrifting.

If you have one weekend to secondhand shop in LA, the following itinerary is what I would send my best friend.

SECONDHAND SHOPPING SPOTS RANKED BY AFFORDABILITY

1. Goodwill Outlet (the bins/any pay-by-the-pound thrift store)
2. Nonprofit thrift stores
3. For-profit thrift stores
4. Estate sales
5. Consignment stores
6. Flea markets
7. Vintage stores

FRIDAY

You're hitting up the most "omg I must get my booty there immediately" estate sale. By the early afternoon there is likely to be little to no line, leaving you with ample time to have plenty of finds at your fingertips. Tap into those tips you learned back in chapter 8 and pop in that Beverly Hills 90210 zip code for the most outrageous estates you have ever seen.

Note: If you are planning a weekend *thriftathon*, I recommend scheduling your spots to shop based first and foremost on affordability. For example, you won't catch me at a more curated spot (like a flea market or vintage store) without checking a few thrift stores or an estate sale first. Take it from me, it's a serious punch to the wallet when you impulse-buy an amazing pair of vintage jeans or leather coat at a more pricey spot, only to then walk into your local thrift and find the exact same or extremely similar item sitting on the rack waiting for you, and, might I add, for less than half the price.

SATURDAY

Snag your thrift totes, grab a coffee (four shots of espresso for me), and head over to the San Fernando Valley! Before I moved to LA, in my naïveté all I knew of the Valley was the infamous Cher Horowitz one-liner in *Clueless*, "Looks like we're going to have to make a cameo at the Val party," but now I know much better. It is honestly fabulous (I recently moved out of the Valley and it pained me to do so) and where I tell everyone to start out their true Los Angeles thrift journey.

Super Thrift in Reseda: This is one of those not-open-on-Sunday type of thrift shops. It's two stories high, with a kids section located upstairs, and I scored a vintage Cavalli dress for $6.99 right off the rack. This is the kind of spot I never leave empty-handed and that will truly give you that real-ass thrifting feel.

Universal Thrift: This spot is cash only but is always having 50 percent off sales, plus it's just a skip down the street from our iconic bestie above, Super Thrift. Universal is one of the most packed thrift stores in town, with double-decker racks of clothing covering the carpet and shelves upon shelves of shoes scattered about.

Note: if you're heading there for home décor, scoot your booty to the upper level, which you will not miss, as the owner gives a full-store rundown as soon as you walk in, every single time.

Hope of the Valley: I cannot say enough good things about this thrift store and organization as a whole. At the core their mission is to prevent, reduce, and eliminate poverty, hunger, and homelessness through their plethora of community programs. They opened this specific location in 2014 and 100 percent of the profits go toward food, clothing, and services for those locally in need. It is MASSIVE. The employees are super kind and I swear, I'm always finding the craziest high-end designer pieces. If you're new to Los Angeles and looking for a thrift store that feels like home, Hope of the Valley will leave you with all the warm fuzzies and iconic hottie finds.

Goodwill: Like I said, if I'm recommending you a Goodwill it's because it's a fucking bop, and this location, less than a mile down from Hope of the Valley, is a must-hit every time.

Secondhand Sundays in LA are for the flea or fleas, depending on how many you can get around to in one day. Here are my favorites.

Rose Bowl Flea: This only occurs on the second Sunday of every month (something to note if you are planning travel!) and is one of the most famous markets in the world, featuring over 2,500 vendors each month. It's definitely on the more pricey side of secondhand shopping but there are plenty of deals to be had in $5–$10 racks and piles. The home décor finds are out of this world.

Silverlake Flea: Silverlake Flea is open every Saturday and Sunday. If you go, you'd be remiss not to also shimmy your way over to **Squaresville Vintage.** LA has a lot of curated vintage shops; you can pretty much throw a rock and hit one holding old band tees from the 1980s, leather boots, and vintage Levi's galore, but if you want something really special with a not-so-heavy price tag, Squaresville is your spot. My best Squaresville scores under $50 have included a Dior blazer, Prada platform sandals, terry-cloth Burberry capri pants, and a vintage Queen tee (an obvious yes-yas).

LA FLEA MARKETS

Long Beach Flea

Los Feliz Flea

Lucky Stars Flea

PCC Swap Meet

Santa Monica Airport Antique Fair

Ventura County Fairgrounds Swap Meet (every Wednesday)

Topanga Flea

Pasadena Flea

Artists and Fleas in Venice

Pickwick Vintage Show

Melrose Trading Post

If you have any gaps left to fill in your days in LA, the shops on **Magnolia Boulevard**, running through Burbank, are a vintage oasis. My favorites include **Playclothes Vintage,** offering a plethora of styles from every decade you may desire. I'm talking from Victorian petticoats to nineties Bebe *hot tops* and every flare, sequin, and shimmy in between.

It's a Wrap is very location-specific, as it's filled with clothing and accessories from Hollywood sets around town. As someone who is so incredibly inspired by TV and film (especially the use of clothing to aid storytelling), I can get lost in this shop for hours.

NEW YORK CITY

I love New York. It's one of the first places where I fell in love with fashion, and the wide range of personal styles that pulse through the veins of those streets provides endless inspiration. However, it is not where I go to really, truly thrift. Of course you can drive out of the city and find the same neighborhood spots as in any other state. However, what the city does have is fabulously curated vintage. Here are the spots I always stop in when I'm having a little New York minute!

Cure Thrift Shop

Goodwill Bins

Le Point Value

Life Vintage and Thrift

Screaming Mimi's

Mother of Junk

Awoke Vintage

L Train Vintage

James Veloria

10 Ft Single by Stella Dallas

Dana Foley

Chickee's Vintage

Urban Jungle Vintage Clothing

Tokio 7

Church Street Surplus

Beacon's Closet

Funny Pretty Nice

Rogue

Seven Wonders Collective

Treasures of NYC

Tired Thrift

MACY'S HOMETOWN BOPS

A few of my home state faves that I feel hold a little extra magic.

Salvation Army (Centerville; first spot I ever thrifted in)

American Thrift

Ohio Thrift

Antiques Village

SPOTS **TO GO ON THE MAP**

ALABAMA

America's Thrift Stores—Center Point

ARIZONA

Turn Style Consignment

Old Habits Vintage—Gilbert

Buffalo Exchange—Tucson (where the Buffalo Exchange originated)

ARKANSAS

Potter's House—Fayette

CALIFORNIA

Valley Oasis Thrift Shoppe—Palmdale (helps victims of domestic violence)

Valley Thrift Store—Escondido

Thrift Center—Fresno

Pikitos—San Francisco

COLORADO

Global Thrift—Denver

Greenwood Wildlife Thrift Shop & Consignment Gallery—Boulder

CONNECTICUT

Mongers Market—Bridgeport

DELAWARE

Goodwill—New Castle County

FLORIDA

Audrey's of Naples—Naples

Red White & Blue Thrift Store—Miami

Zera Outlet—Orlando

Red White & Blue Thrift Store—Tampa

GEORGIA

Lost-n-Found Youth Thrift Store—Atlanta (nonprofit focusing on LGBTQ+ youth)

HAWAII

Aloha Stadium Swap Meet—Honolulu

Vintage Hawaii—Wahiawa

PZAZZ—Honolulu

IDAHO

Thriftology—Boise

Desert Industries—Boise

ILLINOIS

Fulfilled Thrift/Woodstock Community Thrift—Woodstock

Village Discount Outlet—Chicago area

INDIANA

Sell It Here—Lafayette

Thrifty Threads—Indianapolis

Broad Ripple Vintage—Indianapolis

Naptown Thrift—Indianapolis

IOWA

White Rabbit—Iowa City

Found + Formed—Cedar Rapids

Finds Vintage & Retro—Des Moines

The Picker Knows—Des Moines

Brass Armadillo—Des Moines

Crowded Closet—Iowa City

Rumors Vintage—Des Moines

KANSAS

Savers—Overland Park

KENTUCKY

St. Vincent de Paul Louisville Thrift Store—Louisville

New Leash on Life Thrift—Frankfort

Fat Rabbit Thrift & Vintage—Louisville

LOUISIANA

My Faith Thrift Store and Donation Center—Baton Rouge

Mount Grace Thrift Store—Winnfield

Red White and Blue—New Orleans

MAINE

Heavenly Threads—Camden

Freeport Community Services Thrift Shop—Freeport

Lost Coast—Kittery

MARYLAND

2nd Avenue Thrift Stores—Laurel, Baltimore, Columbia

Savers—Adelphi, Brooklyn Park, Landover Hills, Parkville, and Silver Springs

Uptown Cheapskate—Timonium

MASSACHUSETTS

Savers—Boston

Thrift Ave—Hyannis

MICHIGAN

Kiwanis Thrift Sale—near Ann Arbor

Community Thrift Store—Clinton Township

MINNESOTA

Salvation Army—Minneapolis

Goodwill—Minneapolis, Minnetonka

Unique Thrift—Burnsville

Arc's Value Village Thrift Store—Richfield

Clothes Mentor—Adena

MISSISSIPPI

Holding Hands Resale Shop—Oxford

N.U.T.S. (Neat Used Things for Sale)—Jackson

Palmer Home Thrift Stores—Tupelo, Columbus, Starkville

City Thrift—Tupelo

MISSOURI

Snob Shop Exchange—Jefferson

City Thrift—Blue Springs and Kansas City

Boomerang—Kansas City

Thrift World—St. Joseph

Bin Crazy—Springfield

Goodwill Outlet—St. Louis

MONTANA

Reloved Thrift Store—Bigfork

NEBRASKA

Flying Room Vintage—Omaha

NEVADA

Classy Seconds Thrift Shop—Carson City (supports victims of domestic violence)

NEW HAMPSHIRE

Lilise Designer Resale—Concord

NEW JERSEY

Value Village—Hawthorne

American Thrift

MyUnique Thrift Store

Red, White and Blue—Trenton

Pearl Street Consignment—Red Bank

NEW YORK

Thrifty Shopper—multiple locations

Antique World and Flea—Buffalo

Savers—Webster

NORTH CAROLINA

Cause for Paws—Raleigh (kittens to adopt in the store)

Trunkshow—Raleigh

NORTH DAKOTA

Goodwill—Fargo, Grand Forks

Closet Thrift Shop—Bowdon

Arc of Dickinson—Dickinson

OHIO

Plato's Closet—North Olmsted, Strongsville

OKLAHOMA

Donate a Miracle Thriftstore & Boutique—Norman

Goodwill Bins—Oklahoma City

Goodwill—Moore, Tulsa

OREGON

1st Hand Seconds Unique Boutique—Albany (helps women and children affected by domestic abuse)

PENNSYLVANIA

Hey Betty—Pittsburgh

Community Aid Thrift Store & Donation Center—Selinsgrove

Urban Exchange—Philadelphia

Circle Thrift & Circle Thrift Too—Philadelphia

Room Shop Vintage—Philadelphia

Jinxed Fishtown—Philadelphia

Philly Aids Thrift—Philadelphia

RHODE ISLAND

Perennials Consignment—Wakefield

Salvation Army—North Kingstown, Providence

Vault Collective—Providence

Savers—East Providence

SOUTH CAROLINA

Goodwill Bins—Greenville

Kids & More Family Consignment Store—Mauldin

TENNESSEE

City Thrift—Memphis

TEXAS

Family Thrift Center—Houston

Family Thrift Center Outlet—Houston

UTAH

Uncommon—Salt Lake City

Savers—Orem

Lilies of the Field—Salt Lake City

VIRGINIA

Unique—Falls Church

WASHINGTON

Value Village—statewide

Psychic Sisters and Dumpster Values—Olympia

Scorpio Vintage—Tacoma

Evergreen Goodwill—Seattle

WISCONSIN

St. Vincent De Paul Dig & Save Outlet—Madison

WYOMING

NU2U—Laramine

Talk THE TALK

As in any community, the lingo is what bonds us, and if there was ever a word in this book that had you scratching your noggin, let me break down how to talk le talk in my thrifty world. A few of these words are pulled straight from my famously made-up vocabulary, while others are terms necessary in navigating style, as well as life, in a more ethical, sustainable, and inclusive way.

Antique—an item that has aged over one hundred years; however, you will often see this word slapped across the front of a building that contains pieces not quite a century old.

Archive—garments from high-end designers' early collections or anything that feels special and aspirational to you.

Big D's—death, divorce, debt, and downsizing. The ways in which most estate sales come to be.

Bins—wild but fantastic. A culmination of overflow donations, damaged items, and pieces that were on the floor for an extended period of time at a Goodwill store and did not sell. You go, you dig, and everything is likely priced by the pound.

Circularity—a system that minimizes waste by redistributing and reusing resources, such as our favorite place, the thrift store!

Clothing lot—a bulk sum/amount of clothing, usually found on resale sites or auctions. It could be the score of the century, but if you're as lucky as me, it could also be four trash bags full of western wear and square-dancing outfits. You never know.

Cobbler—a magician with a Manolo, mending shoes back to life, through heel tip replacements, strap adjustments, sole revival, and more.

Comps—a pricing tool used by estate sale companies to get an idea of how/what to price that Prada jacket or Pollock painting.

Consignment shop—a whimsical world where clothes turn into cash, or more clothes.

Deadstock—merchandise that either didn't sell or was created in surplus, usually ending up at the thrift store, with their original tags still attached (a true thrift score!).

Digger's paradise—a type of estate sale where chaos is the absolute name of the game.

DIY—"do it yourself." For example, crop a top, paint a table, bedazzle jeans . . . you get the vibe.

Dry cleaner—your vintage afghan coat's best friend. A specialty cleaning service that understands how to clean and care for a plethora of different textiles.

Dry thrift day—when the finds just are not hitting (usually a push from the thrift gods to try out a new spot).

Dumpster diving—literally jumping inside a dumpster to see what you can fish out and give new life to. One person's trash is a thrift queen's treasure. I'm looking at you, stores that throw out perfectly good merchandise.

Dupe—short for duplicate, but in the thrift universe, it's not so copy and paste.

Early bird—one who arrives to shop at the booty-crack of dawn.

Eco-conscious brand—a brand seeking to reduce their environmental impact. Caution: watch out for greenwashing and don't be fooled by an Instagram icon turned green during Earth Month.

Estate sale—a yard sale on speed, usually showcased within a home rather than on the lawn.

Fast fashion—cheap clothing, created in quick response to the latest trends and at the expense of our precious-ass planet.

Fit—an outfit.

Go-back rack—a place where thrift queens hang their unwanted finds for other thrift queens to score.

Goss—gossip, usually of the piping-hot variety.

Gratitudy booty journal—a gratitude journal with a bit of ass. It's a term I made up in 2020 that describes any notebook in which I write down my manifestations and three things I am grateful for daily.

Hot top—a top that makes you feel hot. Hot is a feeling, an inner journey, some may say.

IRL—in real life versus behind a tiny screen.

Like spree—scrolling your secondhand site of choice, throwing a heart or double tap at any item you desire. Best done at night, under the covers, in a melatonin-induced haze.

Mall girl—a girl who was raised on *Laguna Beach*, *That's So Raven*, and Lindsay Lohan, and spent far too much time in Forever 21 between the years 2000 and 2012. Maybe it's you? Maybe it's your mom? Your granddaughter, perhaps? I don't know, but it's definitely me.

Micro trend—the Russian nesting doll of fashion. A trend within a trend within a trend.

Neck test—the not-so-foolproof way of deciphering if a pair of pants will fit. Simply pick up the pants and wrap the waist gently around your neck. Legend has it that if the slacks fit seamlessly around your neck, they will fit well around your waist.

No pile—a collection of treasures curated by a fellow thrift queen. Items they passed up on and graciously left behind for you to score, usually located by the fitting room, the mirrors, or the ends of each rack.

OG—original garment.

Organized chaos—it's messy but it's not.

Pilling—the little balls of lint that pop up on clothes that have been shown a particularly high level of love.

Pinning—saving or uploading images to Pinterest in the process of creating your thrift inspo board.

Poshmark mom—likely an empty-nester on a mission to declutter. Everything must go. The listing is vague, the photos are blurry, but the price is always right.

Ready to wear—pieces created for the general market and sold directly in the store as opposed to made to order for an individual customer.

Real-ass thrift store—endless racks, squeaky hangers, fluorescent lighting, and, possibly, staples used to attach the price tags to the clothes.

Reseller—a controversial liaison of the secondhand world. They dig so you don't have to.

Rework—with a pair of scissors or simple thread, a quilted blanket becomes a patchwork poncho.

Shimmy—shaking your titties or whatever you've got up there with all your might, to summon the fabulous finds!

Size privilege—the idea that people of a certain size, usually what is the societal ideal size or an acceptable size to society, receive certain benefits. In the context of fashion this is something that determines if a customer can fit into the clothing most retailers offer.

Straight size—typically the classic US sizes 0–14, which most traditional retailers carry, despite the average American woman being a size 16.

Sustainability—meeting our current needs without compromising the needs of future generations, while being cognizant and aware of our Three E's from chapter 3: economics, environment, and ethics.

Tag—the key to identifying the age, value, and vibe of your thrift find.

Tailor—a garment shapeshifter; tailors who construct custom pieces, and modify and tailor garments.

Thin privilege—this has nothing to do with whether you perceive yourself to be thin and everything to do with our society being built to the advantage of thin-bodied people.

Thrift and flip—similar to rework, the process of transforming a piece plucked from the rack.

Thrift gods—with no religious affiliation, they are the invisible force that surrounds you as you shop and they are always listening. So say your thrift manifestations out loud so they can deliver!

Thrift haul—my favorite phrase; everything you scored on your secondhand mission.

Thrift manifestation—romanticizing the journey to the find. The epitome of I want it, I thrifted it (see chapter 2 to turn your desires into reality on the rack).

Thrift queen—they're a killer queen . . . at the thrift.

Thriftathon—a thrifting marathon; my absolute personal favorite pastime.

Trend—What's hot? What's now? What are we wearing.

Upcycler—a person who transforms a secondhand item into something totally new, granting it another shimmy around the sun.

Vanity size—the tag says small but it fits like a medium; trust the tape, not the tag.

Vintage—I go by the twenty-plus-years rule, so yes, that does mean your Bebe top from 2002 is now vintage.

Vintage shop—secondhand spots for the more curated shopper. Decades on decades of finds at a price point that matches their worth.

Virtual thrifting—surfing the internet for trends that never reached your town or delving into the "it girl" of your dreams' wardrobe, no matter your geographical location.

Farewell SHIMMIES—from Me to You

I would say we've come to the end of this journey but the truth is you're only getting started! I want to thank you from the bottom of my heart for not only picking up this book but also for opening your mind to the beautiful, magical, and utterly iconic world of giving items, as well as yourself, a second chance.

I wrote this book for the same reason I started sharing my life along with my insane love of thrifting in the first place: to create a space for the "fashion outsiders," to disrupt the "insiders'" ideas of what fashion is or can be, and to invite those not yet on board with secondhand shopping to gain the skills they need to slay.

There can often be this slow burn when it comes to less "conventional" ways of doing things and that definitely applies to our personal buying habits. Society has done quite a good job of convincing us that when we hear the words *old*, *used*, and *worn*, we are talking about something "bad" or useless, and that when we hear the words *new*, *fresh*, and *current*, whatever we're talking about must be "good" or inherently better. We've applied this sentiment to so many facets of our lives and in turn have been left with a pretty big mess. Over the years I've lost count of the times those in my orbit uttered the line, "Is Macy still wasting time doing that thrifting thing?" And each time, I felt their judgment pierce me. I'm sure a lot of you can relate to the particularly crappy feeling that comes from someone shitting on the thing that brings you so much joy. But I beg you to hold on to what makes you happy, because it matters, just like you do.

Writing this book has required a lot of reflecting back on my early thrift days, which were definitely some of the darker points of my life thus far. From 2009 to 2012, any chance I could get, my booty was in the thrift store. I would take my tiny digital camera and make videos, unknowingly practicing for the job I have now. I can't stress enough how influenced (in the best way possible) I was by the people who were scouring the racks right alongside me. Different people, from varying walks of life. Factors like age, gender, or economic bracket were absolutely irrelevant. At the time, I had no idea how monumental and important the conversations I was having with these people would be, whether it was someone my mom's age pulling me aside to relay that when she was a teen she owned the very same top I'd just excitedly scored, the sweet squinting grandpa asking me to read a tag on an item he couldn't quite make out, or the single mother new to this country, needing a little assistance picking out a look for her first job interview. Beyond the amazing fashion finds the thrift store has to offer, the stories that emerged along with the actual purchases themselves are what kept me walking out of those doors, bags in hand, with a smile on my face, every single time.

Secondhand clothing gave me a superhero cloak that granted me the power to express myself long before I had the confidence to shine through my own deepest fears and anxieties. What I found, along with so many others, was the space to be my most authentic self and the access to dream. This book is one of my personal wildest dreams come to life and if I'd given any weight to those who didn't "get it" or see the magic, you definitely wouldn't be reading these words today.

I want you to keep this book tucked tightly in your thrift bag and pull it out when it's time for a wardrobe revamp, you need a "new" look for a night out, there is a must-hit estate sale in your area, or

you simply need some good energy to pull you up and encourage you to keep dreaming and digging for those hot-ass finds!

Discovering the thrift community felt like finding home for the very first time, and I'm so incredibly grateful and excited to be introducing so many new savvy secondhand shoppers to this world.

Remember, truly anything is possible when you take a *second chance*.

ACKNOWLEDGMENTS

THIS BOOK IS MY FIRST EVER DREAM BROUGHT TO LIFE AND WOULD NOT HAVE BEEN POSSIBLE without quite a few fabulous people . . .

Sam Weiner, this book would not exist without you. Thank you for plucking me off the internet and allowing me the most special of spaces to express myself and the ferocious love I have for the secondhand world. You championed my voice, putting complete trust in my vision, and the gratitude I have for that trust is immeasurable. As an extremely anxious Virgo with depression, I am by no means "chill," and throughout this process, while my mind was constantly spinning, you grounded me in my own abilities and always made me feel so empowered to fully express myself. I feel so damn lucky to have had someone as smart, kind, and utterly fantastic at what they do as my editor and lifeline on this (seriously pinch-me moment) journey. You changed my life, and I feel so lucky to have you in my corner. Gina, you are an absolute angel for organizing the crazy amount of images I wanted in this book. Thank you so much for all the work you put into this.

Shubhani, thank you for your incredible patience and being the best book designer a girl with very lofty dreams could wish for. I told you I wanted to create a crazy nod to my favorite childhood magazines, and you made sure every inch of this book reflected what I dreamt up in my mind. You're so amazing, and I cannot thank you enough.

Amy Mazius, it still feels surreal that we got to bring this to life together. Thank you for the countless hours of shooting, brainstorming, laughing, crying, stressing, slaying, repeat!! You captured my world so seamlessly and always got the vibe to a T. My work wife, my bean, and my dream photographer for this project. I love you!

Lexy, my girl. Thank you for being my best friend since the day you popped out of Mom's womb and playing endless hours of dress up with me every single day. You sat by my side as I wrote each chapter, organized the clothing for every shoot, and lent your beautiful mind to these pages whenever I asked. You were the absolute best assistant on this project, and I am so incredibly proud of the woman you have become. You rock so hard, sister bean, and I love you so much!!

Mom, thank you for making me who I am. You are the strongest, bravest, smartest, and most beautiful human I know. When Dad left, you dedicated your life so fully to Lex and I, making sure we always felt loved and enough. Nothing was ever easy, but you made everything the most fun. Thank you for introducing me to every good movie that completely shaped my style and the way I see clothing. You're a superhero and deserve everything good in this world. Danger Girls 4 lyfe!!!

Tyler, my best fucking friend and love of my life. Thank you for getting up with me at the ass crack of dawn every time I want to dig through used clothes in an old home, stopping at every thrift store we ever pass anywhere we ever go, and believing in my biggest dreams since we were teenagers. You and Freddie make my world go round, and I wouldn't be me without you.

My incredible Outfit Equations models, Jamila Stewart, Christen Rhule, Ari Garber, Naythan Cotne, and Lexy Harris, thank you for being your stunning selves. Kevin Hernandez, thank you for taking the most me to the absolute max cover photo! Sin, Brendan Dunlap, Mars, Moe Black, and Carrie Dayton, thank you for sharing your secondhand stories with us via these pages. You're all superstars, and I feel so blessed to have you all a part of the world of *Second Chances*. Anyone and everyone who I interviewed or contributed to this book in any way, thank you thank you THANK YOU from le bottom of my heart.

And little me, thank you for starting this incredible journey for us, being so inspired by the world around you, and finally seeing the magic within yourself.

ACKNOWLEDGMENTS

INDEX